A HOLE IN MY HEART

Finding hope through the seasons of change

AUTUMN ATER

Copyright © 2012 by Autumn Ater. All rights reserved.
ISBN 978-1-938577-01-7

A Hole in My Heart—Finding Hope Through the Seasons of Change
published by **Kouba Graphics Inc., USA**
www.koubagraphics.com

No part of this book may be reproduced or transmitted in any form or by any means, electronic or mechanical, including scanning, photocopying, recording, or by any information storage and retrieval system, without permission in writing from the publisher.

Layout and design by Kouba Graphics, Inc.

10 9 8 7 6 5 4 3 2 1

Dedication

To my wonderful husband Scott.

*For being my best friend and my soul mate,
For being the one I can tell all my secrets to without
judgment and being my greatest supporter.*

*For holding my hand and my heart,
so lovingly and tenderly,
and never letting me give up!*

I love you with each breath I take.

Autumn & Scott Ater

In Loving Memory of
Robert Scott Ater

Our Special Angel
8/12/1991 – 4/22/2006

~Our Precious Boy~

The smile that lit up our lives
now lights up Heaven.
What we keep in memory is ours,
unchanged…forever.

Acknowledgments

To my precious family ~ your love and support is the solid ground with which I stand on. You have encouraged me in so many ways. I thank you for trusting God and having blessed my life.

To the love of my life, Scott, for being the most loving and supportive man I have ever known ~ my best friend and soul mate; who has more patience than anyone I have ever known. I love you with every fiber of my being. You are my heart!

To all the friends in my life whose support I could not have done without. You have all blessed my path.

To my beloved son, Robert, my special angel ~ you've been a gift from God everyday! Your life has always meant something, to me and others. You will never be forgotten.

To all of the special moms who have graced my life with love and compassion. For always lifting me up in prayer and spirit, when I felt as though I was not worthy to lead.

To God the Father, Jesus Christ, my Lord and Savior. Thank You for guiding me and giving me the passion to serve others by serving you. You are an awesome presence in my life.

Table of Contents

Foreword i

Introduction v

1. The day my world seemed to end 1

2. What's happening to me and who am I now? 9

3. Finding our "new normal" 25

4. When others just don't "get it" 35

5. With every passing season 49

6. He walks with me as the journey continues 59

7. I DO have favor with God 73

8. All good deeds 83

9. Praises for His love 99

10. I have a purpose and a plan 109

11. Forgiving grief by enduring it 121

12. Healthy grieving 129

About the Author 147

About "A Hole in My Heart Ministry" 153

Scripture Index 159

*Now that you have purified yourselves
by obeying the truth so that you have sincere love
for each other, love one another deeply,
from the heart.*

Peter 1:22

Foreword
by Susan Duke

There is an unspoken and mysteriously profound connection between Mothers. A silent understanding about a different kind of love. An all encompassing love that finds its empowerment in simply embracing the honor of motherhood itself. But when a mother loses a child, that all powerful-love is rendered powerless in the first waves of grief and helplessness. Beyond our why's is the gripping thought that there is very little in life we truly understand; that our lives will never be the same; and that there will forever be a hole in our heart that will never heal. All of us who have experienced the loss of a child, know all too well those feelings of hopeless despair.

Susan Duke

At some point in our journey, when we realize we can never go backwards or turn back the clock, we have choices to make. *How will we choose to grieve? What do we do with now...and tomorrow?* I truly believe it is in those moments that we embrace

God's plan for the rest of our lives, find the purpose in our pain, honor the gift and legacy of love that will be eternally present, or else become forever trapped beneath the debris of grief's stormy aftermath.

Autumn Ater made her choice. A choice that she would not keep to herself. A choice that would, in a real sense, become the way she honored her precious child, Robert, while at the same time allow her to reach out to the hearts of other mothers in need of help and hope.

Who can say how far reaching one single act of compassion can be? The ripple effect of echoed love finds a voice that is never ending. *A Hole In My Heart Ministry* has become for so many a source of hope in the midst of the storm and a connection in the journey of grief that speaks boldly: *You are not alone.*

In ***Finding Hope Through the Seasons of Change***, Autumn shares authentically and candidly about her own struggles and quest for hope that life can be treasured again. Through stories, practical and spiritual examples, scriptures, poems and quotes relating to where she as well as others have walked, her mother's heart speaks to those places in all of our hearts that yearn for the warmth of comfort and peace.

It is, after all is said and done, our connected journeys that give us faith to share, hope to shine, and love to experience…both in this life and the next.

Foreword

Because forever is happening even now, I pray that Autumn's words will help you know you are not alone and shine a light on your pathway toward healing and the new seasons of your life.

From my own mom's-heart, I pray you will embrace life again and remember every day that love goes on forever.

—Susan Duke
www.suzieduke.com
Author/Speaker

Grieving Forward, Embracing Life Beyond Loss (Time Warner Publishers)

Susan Duke is a wife, mother, bestselling author, inspirational speaker, and singer. A prolific writer, Susan has authored or coauthored 16 books including *Earth Angels, Stories of Heavenly Encouragement Through Earthly Vessels* (Simon & Schuster), *Grieving Forward, Embracing Life Beyond Loss* (Time Warner), *Wolfie's Dream, Wolfie's Christmas Wish* (The Schnauzer Chronicles Series), other titles, poems, devotionals, and articles in over 40 publications.

Susan travels, speaking for Christian conferences, retreats and seminars, corporations, national teacher's associations, community groups, writing conferences (including her own *Writing With Wings* Seminars), and churches of all denominations. An enthusiastic communicator and true encourager, Susan believes life is an adventure to be lived fully. She conveys that message as she combines humor, sensitivity, transparency, and poignant Biblical truth in all of her messages. Her compelling testimony of God's restoration after tragedy offers a bridge of hope for hurting hearts.

In 2002, Susan founded the *Grieving Forward* outreach and support group in her community for anyone experiencing loss. The meetings offer a safe place for grieving hearts to gather and find hope, solace, and support.

Susan's passion for teaching God's Word includes a local Bible Study where ladies meet each month for fellowship and discovering a deeper and more powerful walk with Christ.

Contact Information:
Susan Duke
P.O. Box 8025
Greenville, TX 75404

www.suzieduke.com
suzieduke@juno.com
Facebook/Susan Duke
(903) 883-3355

Introduction

From the first day you grieved your loss, you were already starting on a journey of changing seasons. With each passing day, month and year, these times have brought with them a different perspective; a different way of thinking, feeling and acknowledgment of our loss and the pain that accompanies it.

Each new season brings forth opportunity to come into a closer walk with God, learning a new way to deal with what God's purposes are for our lives. Though we never wanted to go through this unbearable loss, especially that of a child, we are commissioned to love others and trust Him. By reaching out and serving others, we can open a huge door to healing. But only the receptive heart will hear His voice…

We are all given free will, but sometimes that gift conflicts with what we want for our lives. God does have a purpose and a plan, we must be still and listen for His calling and be open to receiving the gifts He has yet to bless us with. He will assist us and provide us with the tools we need to move forward.

We must have an *attitude of gratitude*, which is hard to have when you are dealing with such tragedy and turmoil within. But God will show favor and use the most unlikely vessel. To mention just a couple, remember David (1 Samuel: 17), the youngest son of Jesse who was tending the flock in the pasture and came before King Saul. David was granted permission to fight the Palestine soldier Goliath, who was terrifying to everyone. With one sling, David brought down the mighty Goliath, someone no other could defeat! And then there is Nehemiah (Nehemiah 2), a mere servant who went before the King. Not only did Nehemiah get the King's blessings but he also received all that he asked for ... including the very resources to rebuild the wall of Jerusalem, which should have taken years but was completed in 52 days. Yes, God uses the most unlikely vessel, and shows favor.

We, too, have favor with God. Call upon His name and ask Him what you can do to serve Him. Be a willing vessel. Love and revere Him for He is the one and only true God. Amazing things will happen in your life. You can count on it.

> *We see and experience the glory of God*
> *on the mountain tops ...*
> *but we LIVE IT OUT in the valleys.*
>
> by Gigi Graham Tchividjian

CHAPTER 1

The day my world seemed to end

"What is your life? It is even a vapor that appears for a little time and then vanishes away"

James 4:14

We knew our son, Robert, was sick, and that his days were numbered, but when that dreaded day finally arrived, it still hurt none the less. Just because we knew he would pass at an earlier age did not mean it minimized our pain. In fact, sometimes I think it hurt more knowing all along that his days were numbered. Scripture clearly states this fact:

"For you created my inmost being; you knit me together in my mother's womb. I praise you because I am fearfully and wonderfully made; your works are wonderful, I know that full well. My frame was not hidden from you when I was made in the secret place. When I was woven together in the depths of the earth, your eyes saw my unformed body. All the days ordained for me were written in your book before one of them came to be." Psalm 139:13-16.

Robert had been very sick for 14 plus years and been through many surgeries and illnesses, not to mention the seemingly endless hospital stays, sometimes for weeks at a time only to come home and return again. But I had always been right there by his side, never abandoning him in those darkest times. From the moment he was first diagnosed at 2 ½ months old with a congenital brain malformation called a Migrational Cell Defect, which affected his brain growth and mental development, I was in it for the long haul…but it would ultimately change his and our lives permanently. Then, on a beautiful, sunny Saturday afternoon on April 22, 2006, Robert went home to be with the Lord. All along, I had been his primary care provider and I honestly did not mind that role…but now that he had passed away, I felt as though the life I had known for so long was somehow less important. I had no control anymore of anything and I just didn't seem to fit in anywhere. The world around me was strange and quite frankly, I was scared of how I was going to function.

I wasn't sure of anything anymore…I could not even be alone in my own house. I would spend endless hours at the graveyard, sitting beside his grave and listening to CDs and crying. Oh the oceans I cried there. I just couldn't understand how I had thought I had done everything right for Robert and now he was gone and I was left feeling so alone. Sure I had a wonderful husband at home and an adult daughter with a child of her own living less than five miles away, but I still felt incomplete and useless!

I felt as though I could not breathe, and my very heart physically hurt to beat. I would drop and cry over the smallest of things, a song, a smell, a thought! My sheets were stained with mascara streaks, as I would try to quench the gut wrenching pain inside with never ending tears that just kept coming. Just to look at his photograph now felt strangely odd and painful. At times, I swore I heard him call out 'mama' and I would jump up out of a dazed sleep and go running towards his room, only to find it empty. Just like my heart…just one big empty place, nothing felt alive in me anymore. No, I wasn't prepared for this, not at all. I had the everyday routine down before, but now…I didn't know whether I was coming or going. Nothing seemed real anymore.

I did not know how I was going to survive. I was content in taking care of Robert, now I was lost. I was comfortable in that role. I prayed a lot while dropping huge tears to the ground that sounded like bombs going off as they hit. I would ask God through the tears; *"Why a handicapped child? Why did he have to suffer so? Why was I chosen for this task just to be left feeling this way? What did I do to deserve this? What was the purpose of it all, and why did he have to die?"* These were all legitimate questions I believed I had a right to ask, but I could not hear God at that time through my sorrow. I know other mothers questioned these very same things, asking the 'Why's' of it all... but perhaps not hearing His reply.

I was not mad at God, just confused, which I know Satan was taking total advantage of. He would make me feel such unbearable guilt over Robert's death as we had to play a role in making end-of-life decisions with his doctors, and Satan wanted me to believe that the God I loved and served was just being cruel to me ...punishing me for some unconfessed past sin, and he almost had me convinced. But somewhere in all of his lies, I could hear God calling to me softly, "I am here and Robert is with me. I will never leave you nor forsake you. I love you Autumn. Trust me, as I have your answers and all will be revealed in My timing."

I had always thought that God had created me to be a caregiver—to tend to the needs of a profoundly disabled child, but he started showing me that the day the world I knew of was ending; and was just the beginning of a new journey that He had planned for me all along. He revealed to me that Robert was a vessel as well; one I would come to appreciate on this new path.

God knew that my experiences and willingness to learn all I needed to do to take care of Robert was not to be taken for granted. I was destined for something more than just all of this. And through my pain I was able to find some hope and light at the

Chapter 1: The day my world seemed to end

end of the tunnel and turn my loss into something much more meaningful than living an unfulfilled life of darkness and overwhelming pain.

So yes, a part of my world had ended, but a new world was being formed before my eyes and had only just begun. I just could not see it in the beginning, through tear-filled eyes and a broken heart. But God was preparing me all along for a journey that would not only change my life but that of others who were grieving; respectfully, mothers who had also been through the death of a child or children.

The hole in my heart was going to be filled with many new things, and God kept His promises. He would never leave me or forsake me. He loved me and He was revealing His purposes in all of this. I was ready to receive whatever it was He had planned for me, and I would be obedient to Him as He led the way.

Though there were still going to be numb days and sleepless nights, I knew that life had to go on. "I" had to go on and this was not going to be easy physically, mentally, emotionally or spiritually, but God was going to be calling all the shots now. I was going to go where He led and follow Him. I would trust Him and keep my faith, never letting go of Robert in any way, but allowing him to be a part of the continued plan God had for me. My heart would still ache for Robert and there would be moments where the pain would creep back in, but it was not going to define me or take me away from my obedience to God. He told me He would never leave me and I counted on that, claimed that, and onward I went into the unknown but feeling safe and secure in His care.

As stated by Gina Petner-Ramos in *Soul Survivors, 2/2005*. She says:

You feel you have no more meaning of who you are. You lose yourself. You may have other children around you, but you have no more goals—your original goals are gone. You know you have to move on, but they are a part of your soul—the tragedy brought us somewhere we didn't want to go, so treasure every second! When you lose a child, days are only dark, but there's two ways to deal with it; you are either constructive or destructive. Be constructive...complete their tasks, as it honors them. Learning to accept and understand we will see them again, and that they are always with us even though things went the way they went is powerful stuff. Create a new foundation that honors your child and family. We just gotta move on because there is HOPE!

So, my world did not end…it just changed. And I would have to be determined to put one foot in front of the other, not knowing where they would lead me but trusting that what was about to happen in my life was for the greater good of more than just myself, but for others as well.

Chapter 1: The day my world seemed to end

Although you cannot see me
Don't believe that I am gone;
My spirit still remains
To help you carry on.

Lift your hands to Heaven
And that glimpse of light you see
May be the hope you're seeking
Found inside of me.

A life may wane and wither
And eventually fade from view;
The energy transforms to light
Still to be sensed by you.

Don't assume that I cannot see you
Just because you can't see me;
I'm standing right beside you
Where I always want to be.

Author Unknown

A Hole in My Heart—Finding Hope Through the Seasons of Change

Photo by Cheri with Cherished Memories

CHAPTER 2

What's happening to me and who am I now?

*"Dear friends, do not be surprised
at the painful trial you are suffering, as though
something strange were happening to you.
But rejoice that you participate
in the sufferings of Christ, so that you may be
overjoyed when his glory is revealed."*

1 Peter 4:12-13

I had heard over and over again in the beginning of my loss that "In Christ, all things are made new again" (2 Corinthians 5:17). But I have to admit… at first, I just wasn't feeling it. Not because I didn't want to, or believed it could be so… but because I was trying to discover who I was without my son here anymore and it proved to be a difficult task, one I would definitely need to trust God on.

My roles and titles had changed and were continuing to change and quite frankly, it was awkward. God was leading me into something I knew nothing about, but I was going to be His new creation. Like the butterfly that goes into its cocoon and emerges into this beautiful new being. So I was to be this new being that He was molding into form. I had to trust Him because I could not trust myself. Being flesh, I knew I would fight these changes, and in the midst of all this, I was still grieving the death of my son… but He; (God) spoke to me. He directed His voice to the very core of my soul and I was listening.

As he spoke to me, I did hear Him. He told me that I would serve others, by continuing the ministry He had started within me in obedience to His will. He was planting a seed into a mothers broken heart and there, along with her (my) tears and that of other women, He would water the seed and spread forth its tendrils to entwine with the hearts and hurts of other bereaved mothers. He was direct and to the point, no debate!

Some have asked me, when God planted the seed for ministry into your heart, did you hear His voice or thunder? What did He sound like? All I can tell you is that when He speaks to you, you will know it. There was no thunder or unfamiliar sound. On the contrary, He sounded beautiful and full of purpose. You just know that it is the great "I AM" speaking to you and you get what many refer to as the Holy Ghost bumps. I never questioned what I heard that late night lying there in my own tears once again, while in prayer, but instead, I jumped into action. I WAS going to be obedient to Him and He was going to create something so wonderful and so needed that

Chapter 2: What's happening to me and who am I now?

it would touch the lives of many. It was on that night that *"A Hole in My Heart Ministry"* was born.

Sitting there at my computer in the wee hours of the morning, less than a year after Robert's death, He led my fingers as they typed out the rough draft for the ministry. Every scripture, every word, every detail was placed there by Him. I was a vessel and He was using me without any hesitation.

In less than two weeks, things were going fast. A website was established; www.aholeinmyheart.com thanks to the talents and skills of my daughter Elaina, brochures were created and printed and off they went. Contacts were made to all the local churches, funeral homes, hospices and hospitals. The newspaper was contacted and an article was done. Within just a short week's time, over 30 contacts came in from mothers all over the area, wanting more information and to know where we would meet and when. It was a bit overwhelming to say the least, but I went to my pastor and he was 100% on board in excitement. He offered the use of the church and its facilities, and asked for volunteers to help and assist where needed. He and his wife had the opportunity to come and see Robert just a week before his passing and had knelt at the steps of the church's alter many times with me after Robert's death to comfort me and pray with me. So it meant a lot to me that they supported this vision God had planted in me.

So now, I am the founder of a wonderful organization that reaches mothers locally, nationally and internationally. We have grown to great numbers and women welcome the quarterly newsletters, monthly meetings, annual mother's retreats, and additionally, along with their families in attendance; our annual butterfly releases and holiday candle lighting memorials.

In April 2011, a beautiful Fountain and statue of Mary holding baby Jesus was placed at Praise Pavilion of Weatherford, TX (www.praisepavilion.org) which is open year round, 24/7 for anyone who would like to visit. Leading up to "The Fountain of Tears" are bricks inlaid with the names of our children and messages, affectionately called, "The Prayer Walk." It is a most humble and tranquil; Holy place, and all who visit there leave with a renewed sense of peace and hope!

I have a new purpose, a new role. I have a new identity, one that is in Christ and I am made new again. I am humbled by all that God has brought to my life, even this being my second book. You know, I am amazed at how God continues to bless me and A Hole in My Heart Ministry. I stood in front of the mirror and thought, "Who am I that God has shown such favor and blessings upon? That He would bless me with Robert, carry me through his life and his death, plant the seed for ministering to other mothers, place a custom statue and fountain in a most beautiful setting and write two books?" Wow, it's almost overwhelming but at the same time, honoring! To think, when I am no longer here on earth, all this still remains of my work for the Lord! It's truly incredible. God does not take our work lightly and, He knows our heart!

I love the following scripture:

> *O LORD, you have examined my heart*
> *and know everything about me.*
> *You know when I sit down or stand up.*
>
> *You know my thoughts even when I am far away.*
> *You see me when I travel and when I rest at home.*
>
> *You know everything I do. You know what I am*
> *going to say even before I say it, LORD.*
> *You go before me and follow me.*
>
> *You place your hand of blessing on my head.*
> *Such knowledge is too wonderful for me,*
> *Too great for me to understand!*
> *I can never escape from your Spirit!*
>
> *I can never get away from your presence!*
> *If I go up to Heaven, you are there;*
> *If I go down to the grave, you are there.*

*If I ride the wings of the morning,
if I dwell by the farthest oceans,
even there your hand will guide me,
and your strength will support me.*

*I could ask the darkness to hide me
and the light around me to become night
but even in darkness I cannot hide from you.
To you the night shines as bright as day.
Darkness and light are the same to you.*

*You made all the delicate, inner parts of my body
and knit me together in my mother's womb.
Thank you for making me so wonderfully complex!*

*Your workmanship is marvelous—how well I know
it. You watched me as I was being formed in utter
seclusion, as I was woven together in the dark
of the womb. You saw me before I was born.*

*Every day of my life was recorded in your book.
Every moment was laid out before
a single day had passed.*

*How precious are your thoughts about me, O God.
They cannot be numbered! I cannot even count
them; They outnumber the grains of sand!
And when I wake up, You are still with me!*

Psalm 139: 1-18

This is so healing to think about. He does love us, no matter what our circumstances or trials. He knows our beginning and our end and He guides us through each part of our walk! Amen!

God is an ever present part of our journey. He will never abandon us or leave us, for we belong to Him. I am honored to serve our Lord in serving these precious women whose paths have crossed mine. Wonderful divine appointments as I call them.

My walk with the Lord has matured and grown over the past six years. We recently observed Robert's sixth year "angelversary" and yet it is six years closer to being reunited with him again. Although my mother's heart will always miss him, I have the truth, knowledge and promise from the father that we will see each other again…no more goodbyes. Not ever. A thousand years is but a day! That is like the thought, before the thought, before the thought of the thought that your eye will blink… times another thousand. There is no measure of time with God. How wonderful will it be to be in His presence and that of Jesus, and our precious children for all of eternity?

I have found that what happened to me did not define my complete purpose or being, but who I am now which is a stronger person who is in a loving relationship with Christ. I hope that you, too, find who you truly are and that by letting your grief identify you as anything other than a vessel for God or as being created for a purposeful relationship with the Father is Satan putting lies into your head. You must rebuke him in the name of Jesus and move forward. There is hope!

As written by The Grief Toolbox, "Grief can make us feel very lonely. Sometimes we need to be alone with our feelings and our thoughts. Other times we need others to listen and share with us so that we realize that we are not alone on our journey. Others have been where we are, they have felt the excruciating pain, the long lonely nights, the confusion and survived. Find these people, if not among your own family or friends then with a support group. You will find hope in hearing others share their journey and soon you will help others find hope by sharing your journey."

I knew when I read these three passages in "A Journey with God Beyond Grief," by Dr. Criswell Freeman, PsyD, that I had heard God himself speaking to me, through another vessel, and this is what I read and heard:

1. *God has an important plan for your life; and part of His plan may well be related to your grief. Your suffering carries with it great potential: the potential for intense personal growth and the potential to help others. As you begin to reorganize your life, always be watchful for ways*

Chapter 2: What's happening to me and who am I now?

to use your suffering for the betterment of others. As a wounded survivor, you will have countless opportunities to serve others, and by serving others, you will bring glory to God and meaning to the suffering you have endured. Dr. Criswell Freeman, PsyD.

2. *The grace of God is sufficient for all our needs, for every problem and for every difficulty, for every broken heart, and for every human sorrow. —Quote by Peter Marshall.*

3. *Be not afraid, only believe. Mark 5:36.*

I now knew that He had planted a seed worth tending! And tending to it was what I was going to do. I could not be more humbled or honored to do this work for Him. And even in all this, I knew that Satan would try to come and steal my joy on many occasions, but I have been equipped with a supernatural protector… Jesus Christ, and Satan cannot touch this ministry for he is bound then by the name of Jesus and with that I can move forward with doing His work. I belong to Him; what joy! Praises, Praises and more Praises!

I found the following article of information so helpful from Dr. Alan D. Wolfelt, who is a noted author, educator and practicing grief therapist. He is the Founder and Director of the Center for Loss and Life Transition in Fort Collins, Colorado. He states the following most educational information:

Helping Yourself Heal When Your Child Dies

Allow Yourself to Mourn

Your child has died. You are now faced with the difficult, but important, need to mourn. Mourning is the open expression of your thoughts and feelings regarding the death of your child. It is an essential part of healing.

With the death of your child, your hopes, dreams and plans for the future are turned upside down. You are beginning a journey that is often frightening, painful and overwhelming. The death of a child results in the most profound bereavement. In fact, sometimes your feelings of grief may be so intense that you do not understand what is happening. This brochure provides practical suggestions to help you move toward healing in your personal grief experience.

Realize Your Grief is Unique

Your grief is unique. The unique child you loved and cared for so deeply has died. No one, including your spouse, will grieve in exactly the same way you do. Your grief journey will be influenced not only by the relationship you had with your child, but also by the circumstances surrounding the death, your emotional support system and your cultural and your religious background.

As a result, you will grieve in your own unique way. Don't try to compare your experience with that of others or adopt assumptions about just how long your grief should last. Consider taking a "one-day-at-a-time" approach that allows you to grieve at your own pace.

Allow Yourself to Feel Numb

Feeling dazed or numb when your child dies may well be a part of your early grief experience. You may feel as if the world has suddenly come to a halt. This numbness serves a valuable purpose: it gives your emotions time to catch up with what your mind has told you.

You may feel you are in a dream-like state and that you will wake up and none of this will be true. These feelings of numbness and disbelief help insulate you from the reality of the death until you are more able to tolerate what you don't want to believe.

This Death is Out of Order

Because the more natural order is for parents to precede their children in death, you must readapt to a new and seemingly illogical reality. This shocking reality says that even though you are older and have been the protector and provider, you have survived while your child has not. This can be so difficult to comprehend.

Not only has the death of your child violated nature's way, where the young grow up and replace the old, but your personal identity was tied to your child. You may feel impotent and wonder why you couldn't have protected your child from death.

Expect to Feel a Multitude of Emotions

The death of your child can result in a variety of emotions. Confusion, disorganization, fear, guilt, anger and relief are just a few of the emotions you may feel. Sometimes these emotions will follow each other within a short period of time. Or they may occur simultaneously.

As strange as some of these emotions may seem, they are normal and healthy. Allow yourself to learn from these feelings. And don't be surprised if out of nowhere you suddenly experience surges of grief, even at the most unexpected times. These grief attacks can be frightening and leave you feeling overwhelmed. They are, however, a natural response to the death of your child. Find someone who understands your feelings and will allow you to talk about them.

Be Tolerant of Your Physical and Emotional Limits

Your feelings of loss and sadness will probably leave you fatigued. Your ability to think clearly and make decisions may be impaired. And your low energy level may naturally slow you down. Don't expect yourself to be as available to your spouse, surviving children, and friends as you might otherwise be.

Respect what your body and mind are telling you. Nurture yourself. Get daily rest. Eat balanced meals. Lighten your schedule as much as possible. Caring for yourself doesn't mean feeling sorry for yourself, it means you are using survival skills.

Talk About Your Grief

Express your grief openly. When you share your grief outside yourself, healing occurs. Ignoring your grief won't make it go away; talking about it often makes you feel better. Allow yourself to speak from your heart, not just your head. Doing so doesn't mean you are losing control or going "crazy." It is a normal part of your grief journey.

Watch Out for Cliches

Cliches—trite comments some people make in attempts to diminish your loss can be extremely painful for you to hear. Comments like, "You are holding up so well," "Time heals all wounds," "Think of what you have to be thankful for" or "You have to be strong for others" are not constructive. While these comments may be well-intended, you do not have to accept them. You have every right to express your grief. No one has the right to take it away.

Develop a Support System

Reaching out to others and accepting support is often difficult, particularly when you hurt so much. But the most compassionate self-action you can do at this difficult time is to find a support system of caring friends and relatives who will provide the understanding you need. Seek out those people who encourage you to be yourself and acknowledge your feelings—both happy and sad.

A support group may be one of the best ways to help yourself. In a group, you can connect with others who have experienced the death of a child. You will be allowed and gently encouraged to talk about your child as much, and as often, as you like.

Sharing the pain won't make it disappear, but it can ease any thoughts that what you are experiencing is crazy, or somehow bad. Support comes in different forms for different people—find out what combinations work best for you and try to make use of them.

Embrace Your Treasure of Memories

Memories are one of the best legacies that exist after the death of your child. You will always remember. Instead of ignoring these memories, share them with your family and friends. Keep in mind that memories can be tinged with both happiness and sadness. If your memories bring laughter, smile. If your memories bring sadness, then it's all right to cry. Memories that were made in love—no one can take them away from you.

Gather Important Keepsakes

You may want to collect some important keepsakes that help you treasure your memories. You may want to create a memory book, which is a collection of photos that represent your child's life. Some people create memory boxes to keep special memories. Then, whenever you want, you can open up your memory box and embrace these special memories. The reality that your child has died does not diminish your need to have these objects. They are a tangible, lasting part of the special relationship you had with your child.

Embrace Your Spirituality

If faith is part of your life, express it in ways that seem appropriate to you. Allow yourself to be around people who understand and support your religious beliefs. If you are angry at God because of the death of your child, realize this feeling as a normal part of your grief work. Find someone to talk with who won't be critical of whatever thought and feelings you need to explore.

You may hear someone say, "With faith, you don't need to grieve." Don't believe it. Having your personal faith does not insulate you from needing to talk out and explore your thoughts and feelings. To deny your grief is to invite problems that build up inside you. Express your faith, but express your grief as well.

Move Toward Your Grief and Heal

To restore your capacity to love, you must grieve when your child dies. You can't heal unless you openly express your grief. Denying your grief will only make it become more confusing and overwhelming. Embrace your grief and heal.

Reconciling your grief will not happen quickly. Remember, grief is a process, not an event. Be patient and tolerant with yourself. Never forget that the death of child changes your life forever.

You can't live a positive life in a negative mind.

Anonymous

CHAPTER 3
Finding our "new normal"

*...to be made new in the attitude of your minds;
and to put on the new self, created to be like God
in true righteousness and holiness.*

Ephesians 4:23-24

What does a new normal mean? And how in the world do you find it? For those of us who have been given this new title, it's quite frightening. We still want to be ourselves and we don't want to be this new normal thing, or person people keep telling us we have to be. But, we are different now. We are still the same person inside, minus our loss of course, but it's that minus that changes everything about who we once were and who we are going to now be.

At the finale of the movie; "Eat, Pray, Love," I heard these words being spoken by the character that Julia Roberts portrayed:

"In the end, I've come to believe in something I call the physics of the quest—a force in nature governed by laws as real as the laws of gravity. The rules of quest physics goes something like this:

If you're brave enough to leave behind everything familiar and comforting, which can be anything from your house, your old life, even some bitter old resentments, and set out in a truth-seeking journey either externally or internally; and if you are truly willing to regard everything that happens to you on that journey as a clue; and if you accept everyone you meet along the way as a teacher; and if you are prepared most of all to face and forgive some very difficult realities about yourself, then the truth will not be withheld from you.

I can't help but believe it, given my experiences. So, let's cross over (to a new self/new life)."

I found this to be quite a revelation. It spoke volumes to my understanding of what this new normal really is. It is not something I ever asked to become but I was going to have to learn something from it. I was going to have to become fearless, brave hearted, strong and accept the things that I cannot change. I was going to have to let go of some of me and my past hurts, dreams and hopes to become prepared to face the inevitable truth; which was that my son had died and I was going to have to move on. I would appreciate and respect those sent onto the path with me in hopes of learning this new normal lifestyle without resentment. And I was going to find, based on my life's experiences, a new joy in this new person I was becoming.

Everyone finds their new normal lifestyle somewhere along life's path, when and where that will happen is something I cannot answer for anyone but myself. My choice was to become something new now—to allow God's love to flow through me and reach out to others with that same intense power to find a way to love back. To offer something from my own loss in hopes that it would help someone else who was suffering this great pain as well. I was not going to be immune to feeling my pain, I was just going to become strong enough to use it to glorify God and do His will. Would I be able to reach anyone? Would I be helpful? Would I even know what to say when the moment came? God said yes! He showed me in Romans 8:26;

"In the same way, the Spirit helps us in our weakness. We do not know what we ought to pray for, but the Spirit himself intercedes for us through wordless groans."

I knew I had been given the answer. It wasn't going to be me that knew what to say, not beyond my own knowledge of loss anyhow, but that of God's intervening. He was going to provide me with the tools I would need to reach these humbled and broken hearts, wounds so deep that only He could understand the true depth of it all, for He is God... the creator of all living things, both here and in Heaven. My new normal was going to transform me into the creation that He had designed me to be, before I ever came to be, He knew He had chosen me for this very task. Now it was not a matter of my will…but His.

Be reminded, grief is a process. Not a 12-step program that you attend meetings to complete and now are made well again. It's a life long process of rediscovering the newness of each day and what would be brought to it and out of it. It was seeing the morning sun and thanking God for a new day. It was seeing the stars blanketing the night sky and the moon and thanking God for the days end. No promise of tomorrow, just a hope that there would be one. It was hearing the birds sing out, seeing a butterfly swoop by, seeing the smile on a child's face, holding hands with the one you love, reading a letter from an old friend or cuddling up with your favorite blanket, a good book and your precious little lap dog and being thankful. Just thankful!

As quoted by the well known photographer, Dewitt Jones, *"A bird sings not because it has an answer—but because it has a song. It's not just about trying to make a difference, but a contribution."* Reaching out to others during this time will reap many benefits to your healing process, making a difference in how you heal from your loss. It is finding beauty and serenity in the living and the world around us once again.

The challenge will be great for many and some will have to go to the valley and be very still and very

Chapter 3: Finding our "new normal"

quiet; and listen for His voice. Hear His majesty in the wind and feeling it brush against your face as though His hand was gently stroking your cheek and knowing there is more than just all of this. He is here with us, He reminds us everyday. We just have to get still, listen, feel and accept His mighty love for us.

In this insert, I found such truth's about how I was feeling... "When will I get relief? Will this empty feeling ever go away? Am I ever going to get over this loss?" What we're really trying to say is, "I wish this never happened, and I want to turn back the clock and go back to how things were before this loss."

But, the world as we once knew it no longer exists. Our grief experience has changed life as we once knew it forever. We now live in a new place, and it's up to us to work very hard to find a new normal. Yet, we still keep on trying to turn the clock back. We keep wishing and hoping and remembering. The pain feels like it is just too much!

As written by Clara Hinton:

Little by little, though, hope begins filtering in through the cracks in our heart and brain, and we realize that even though our world is now totally different, we must find a way to go on. We begin to establish new traditions, find new ways to place peace in our souls, and we realize that we really aren't alone at all.

Hope pushes us forward even when we feel like we can't go on. Hope helps us to see the beauty in small things such as a smile, a babbling brook, or a gentle snowfall. We understand more fully how to cherish the small moments in life, and we are so thankful for every ray of sunshine that touches our heart. Hope is alive, and hope teaches us how to live again!

"A hopeful heart is a peace-filled heart."

> *"The Lord of hosts is with us."*
> Psalm 46:7

Although the burden will lighten over time, there will still be moments of deep sadness, frustration, lack of understanding, panic and brokenness and with all that, more tears, but we need to keep moving forward and not let our grief identity us or our purpose! It's not easy by any means, nor is it meant to be. We can only deal with each moment as it comes and be ready to face the fact that another will eventually follow in how we feel. This is one thing that will take us our lifetime to reflect over, but I know in my faith that HE does walk this long and painful journey with us. I also believe that we will be reunited with our children again in HIS timing. Until then, we must run the good race towards the prize which is awaiting us.

The new normal that I long to be is the one that He purposes and declares me to be. The one that will hear His voice and calling and answer;

"Yes Father, I hear you. I am yours and I will trust you and follow you. I am nothing without you Lord, not even my next breath comes unless you say it to be so, and I will love you with all my heart and be your servant. I will accept in my heart that you will direct my paths, protect me and lead, guide and direct me as I go forth."

This is a part of the new normal that I need to become, that I want to become. It will complete me and allow me to leave behind more than the legacy of family, but work done to serve a wonderful and awesome God. I will not be afraid, *Isaiah 41:10* states:

So do not fear, for I am with you;
do not be dismayed, for I am your God.
I will strengthen you and help you;
I will uphold you with my righteous right hand.

Now that's the God that I want to serve and transform me into a new creation; to fill me with His wisdom and His knowledge. He will never fail me in this new normal state of being.

There is yet another perspective to our grieving cycle that I must cover as a part of our New Normal as shared in, *"The Social Intelligence"* by Goleman, and which was a part of a Bible study with Beth Moore and Grief Share. It states that the grieving cycle consists of the following attributes: Shock, Denial, Bargaining, Anger, Worry, Depression,

Relief, Acceptance and Action. We must learn to honor our emotions. The normal range to any loss is change. Each topic brings with it questions that only you can ask pertaining to your specific situation regarding loss though. We must remember that life does not stop, but when it compresses and intensifies to a boiling point, this is where you may find you need to seek additional help through counseling. Panic and fear only stops actions which lead to peace, hope and a new normal attitude.

There is a transition curve to a New Normal which shows; Denial (numbness), Resistance (fear of changes), Exploration (uncertain/chaos) and Commitment (renewed hope). Starting from past to future, we see this curve swooping down and back up around within our external environment. These are those reflections of grief.

There are four phases of change:

1. ***Denial***, which is an effort by the individual to hold on to the ways things were. Your first reaction will be to feel numbness. You find you are in a state of pretense that nothing has happened. Often times, people who are in denial may not be upset because they stay focused on the way things were (neglecting both themselves and their future), not exploring how they feel or need to change.

2. ***Resistance*** is when one has moved from denial and numbness and begins to experience

lower self-esteem, anger, depression, anxiety, frustration or fear because of the change. This causes people to resist the change. They will now focus on personal impact of the change and on what they will lose as a result of the change rather than what they might gain. They believe they are isolated, alone and that no one else understands, and that their feelings and reactions are more intense than anyone else's.

3. *Exploration* is the acceptance beginning within. When acceptance begins, people identify with the change and realize they have a stake in the success of their future. This is a time of high energy, but unfocused ideas. Another word for this phase is chaos! Although many things are in question, uncertain, and stressful, people will tend to draw on their internal creative energy to figure out ways to capitalize on the future. This phase can be exciting, exhilarating, and fun.

4. *Commitment* is when one has accepted the changes and are ready to focus on a plan. A renewed sense of hope and commitment is being felt, and a true sense of purpose and direction toward a new beginning. One is likely to now begin these new ventures with plans that are attainable. There is general sense of relief and well-being now. Those who are committed are now looking for the next new challenge.

These are all helpful tools in discovering a way to manage your grief and finding your new normal. You will need to continuously ask yourself questions on a daily basis, such as:

> *How is my life in general?*
> *Where am I emotionally, physically,*
> *spiritually, and relationally?*

These are all very important questions, and one I will add which has helped me in finding who I am in this new normal which is:

> *What can I do to help/comfort someone else*
> *that would be pleasing to God?*

Now we have covered an outline for better knowledge of what we must decide upon. Will we stay a victim to our loss or be a victor? I choose to be the latter and move with determination that God is using me for a greater purpose. Will you?

I leave you with this quote by Emily Dickinson, which states;

> *"Hope" is the thing*
> > *with feathers that perches in the soul*
> > > *and sings the tune without words*
> > > > *and never stops—at all.*

CHAPTER 4
When others just don't get it

*Let them be like chaff before the wind,
with the angel of the Lord driving them away!*

Psalm 35:5

In finding our new normal lifestyle, we who have suffered the loss of a child, have all had those come to us in our time of need and spout out things that just frustrate us. Some will share words that will help us, others that will hurt us.

I remember someone saying to me at Robert's funeral, "Oh I know just how you feel; I just lost my little dog a week ago." In my mind, I am like, what??? Did she just compare the death of my child to her dog? Yep, she sure did! I am sure she was grieving over her pet, but to compare it to the loss of my son was absurd. How could you compare it? You cannot. Unless you have suffered this loss and are trying to move forward in your new world, a comment like that can haunt you.

Many have told young mothers and fathers, "Well, you're still young, you can have more children." Like as if to say, it's no big deal, you can always have another baby…NOT! No, not even close. You can never replace the life you lost and for someone to think we should just get on with our lives and act as though nothing has happened, is ludicrous.

There are some that will not want to talk to you about your loss; yes, this is where ignorance is bliss. They don't understand, and thank God because you wouldn't want them to, but they say all sorts of things that just make you cringe inside. If you haven't ever experienced this particular type of loss, you cannot possibly "get it." We know that perhaps they mean well, but when someone states that it's been six months and it's time to move on…you almost want to physically lunge at their face, because you feel slapped in yours. How can people be so insensitive? And what about the ones who have suffered the loss of a child and start instructing people to get over it? There is nothing short of denial going on here, or something worst. We shutter to think someone could be so cruel or cold hearted when we are doing all we can just to move one foot in front of the other.

Recently, a friend of mine, Vickie Warrington Davis, made a comment that has really stirred me. What she said is so true and incredibly awesome. Please read:

Grief is a Monster. It comes in the dark like a bad dream; it comes during the day like a robbery. We are all affected by our grief, we are all individuals but on the same path. If there is someone grieving differently than you, please know we do not grieve the same. We all need to know we are cared about and respected. Sometimes a kind word or action can mean so much, not judgment. A recipe we all know we might doctor up a bit and make it our way, this reminds me of grief. It is ours... I deeply care for you all and if I can, I will help, but like you; I may need help sometimes, too. We all walk the same road. Let's take hands on this journey!

When someone confronts you in a way that is hurtful or innocently ignorant, remind them of this letter written by Margaret Brownley:

Dear Friend,

Please be patient with me; I need to grieve in my own way and in my own time.

Please don't take away my grief or try to fix my pain. The best thing you can do is listen to me and let me cry on your shoulder. Don't be afraid to cry with me. Your tears will tell me how much you care.

Please forgive me if I seem insensitive to your problems. I feel depleted and drained, like an empty vessel, with nothing left to give.

Please let me express my feelings and talk about my memories. Feel free to share your own stories of my loved one with me. I need to hear them.

Please understand why I must turn a deaf ear to criticism or tired clichés. I can't handle another person telling me that time heals all wounds.

Please don't try to find the "right" words to say to me. There's nothing you can say to take away the hurt. What I need are hugs, not words. Please don't push me to do things I'm not ready to do, or feel hurt if I seem withdrawn. This is a necessary part of my recovery. Please don't stop calling me. You might think you're respecting my privacy, but to me it feels like abandonment. Please don't expect me to be the same as I was before. I've been through a traumatic experience and I'm a different person.

Please accept me for who I am today. Pray with me and for me. Should I falter in my own faith, let me lean on yours. In return for your loving support, I promise that, after I've worked through my grief, I will be a more loving, caring, sensitive, and compassionate friend—because I have learned from the best.

Love, Me

Now that should help put them in the right perspective and be better able to help you. We all grieve differently and we can't expect them to understand but we can guide them in a more positive direction. It will be less awkward for everyone that way. Another good thought is from Nancy Guthrie's newsletter, dated June 2009.

When you're feeling stuck in your grief...

The only way I found I could move forward was to dig deeper into God's Word to learn more about his character so that I could trust him, and to invest my energy and focus as much as possible in people around me who are living and need me rather than giving all of my focus and energy to my grief. As a mom, I also had to keep telling myself the truth; that it is not a betrayal of my children to choose joy, that my love for them is not defined by my ongoing misery. Written by Nancy Guthrie.

We cannot let our grief, painful as it is, identify our lives. God creates divine appointments with those he will place in our path who will encourage us and more importantly *accept* us for who we are. Though we will always miss our child, we must remember that they are with us in spirit and God is protecting and watching over them, and us...even when we cannot feel their presence with us, they are there, in our hearts, forever. And God loves us through it all, forever and ever!

Child, my child; My sun, my moon
Child, my child; My day, my night;

One day I will find you; Wherever you are
You went to sleep forevermore
No more pain; Forever at peace.

We cherish your memory and send our love
On wings of wind; My child, my angel
Heaven is your home.

Lord, until we meet again
Take care of my angel for me.

Author Unknown

I think we have all heard someone say to us at some point in time, "God loves you." And sometimes we've probably wondered, "Is that actually true? Does God really love me? How can I be sure?" because some people who claim to be Christians have really let me down and that's not love to me…

Grief causes many reactions in others. It's as if it is an almost fearful emotion to them, and they don't want to "catch it." Maybe you've been let down and terribly disappointed by people. Maybe someone said that he or she loved you and then turned against you. Maybe someone said that he or she was your closest friend, but ultimately betrayed you. Maybe they even walked with you in your grief but found they just couldn't go the distance and left us to carry on by ourselves. This happens all too often for the grieving parent. When it comes to God's love, we tend to ask ourselves whether it is for real as well. We wonder whether He, too, will turn away from us if we let Him down by falling apart in our grief. But, Jesus is God demonstrating His love for His own.

He knows the abandonment and betrayal we have felt or may now be feeling as he, too, suffered this situation as well.

My friend, Summer, recently commented:

To speak to anyone about your deepest emotions while they try to help you pick through them, sort them out, it is just mind numbing. To dedicate your morning to prayer and to dive into the word of God so intimately, yes it is comforting, but it is not an easy task. The warfare spreads like wildfires and my armor just drags behind me...I am so tired. My head aches, my body is sore, I feel as if I just left the battlefield, the realization of this is that the battle has only just begun.

Grieving is not for the weak. Tackling these emotions head on everyday takes strength, it takes courage if you ever think that someone who grieves for another must be weak, you are so very wrong and I pray no one I know will ever have to experience tragedy of any sort like this.

Friends of those grieving can play a healthy or unhealthy part of our loss. What do you do or say to be a better comfort and friend? With permission, from a heart-wrenching and outstanding article in a wonderful support ministry for bereaved parents; Grief Haven (www.griefHaven.org), this following message comes to help others learn a way to be a better friend when there are no words to say:

Ten Commandments for close friends of newly grieving parents by Margaret Balian.

1. *Get help now*—There is a way that works and a way that doesn't work when supporting your grieving friend. You most likely have no idea what does work. How can you know? But there are those who do know, so contact someone who can enlighten you. If you have done something that hurt your friend, instead of reacting negatively, which only makes matters worse, contact someone who can tell you how to get it right. A support group is a great place to start. See a grief counselor. Read a book. Do what you have to do to be there for your friend, and get the support you need in the process. No one expects you to know how, but finding out is so easy.

2. *Stop, look, and listen*—**STOP** and think before speaking to your friend. Realize that you do not need to "fix" your friend because there is nothing wrong with her. She is grieving, and that is what she needs to do. That grief goes on for a very long time. I learned that most parents cry every day for a year or more. Resist the urge to fill the silence with chatter. A simple, "I'm so sorry" is often best. Your friendship and presence mean everything. Take it in and just *be* in that sad space as your friend grieves. Don't try to talk your friend out of how she feels or point out all the good things in life. Just let it be. She will eventually find her way.

LOOK around. If you are visiting your grieving friend, what is around you that might be a hurtful reminder? A car seat? Then remove it before you arrive. If she is coming to your home, ask her ahead of time if there is anything you can do to make her visit a little easier, such as put toys away or have a photo of your friend's child out. I was told that it is a good idea to ask your friend if there is anything she would like. If she says she doesn't know, then give her some specific options. Just know that she will appreciate the fact that you cared enough to ask.

LISTEN to what your friend has to say about her grief and her child. Don't point out all the good things about her life or her child when she's sharing. Don't change the subject because you are uncomfortable or think talking about something else will help her. Having you there listening is what helps her. Let her cry, and, if it comes up naturally for you, you cry, too. I've learned that parents are not upset when someone cries when in their presence. The fact that you are there for them is what is important. They need their friends and loved ones now more than ever before.

3. ***Realize it's not personal***—The rules have changed. This is not your old friendship, and it is not an equal friendship. Their child died; yours (if you have any) are alive and healthy. They need

time to process, and they need your support. You give; they receive. You have other friends that can fill your "normal" friendship needs. This is not the time nor the place to put your needs first. Rise above! One day, they might want to talk to Friend A but not Friend B. Celebrate the fact that they are connecting with someone…anyone.

4. ***Stay in their lives***—Let them know you are thinking about them on a regular basis. Even if you can't visit, a simple text to say you are thinking of them and that you love them will mean a lot. Some friends will not feel like visiting or receiving calls, but a loving thought is always welcomed. An example might be, "I'm just checking in and wanted you to know I was thinking about you" or "I love you. I love (insert child's name)." If they share something painful and you don't know what to say, try "I'm so sorry." Don't avoid connecting for days or weeks.

5. ***Say good-bye to every platitude you ever learned***—Those platitudes that are way overused and do not help even a little bit need to be erased from all of our memories. Comments like, "He/she is in a better place," "Time heals all wounds," "You need to get out and stay busy," and "At least they're not in pain anymore" only add heartache to an already broken heart. If you speak from a loving and compassionate place, you will be in safe territory. For instance, you can say, "Just

Chapter 4: When others just don't get it

thinking of you," "I cannot imagine how you feel," "My heart breaks for you," "I wish I knew what to say or do, but I don't," and "Even though I don't know what to say or do, I don't want to avoid you for fear of saying or doing the wrong thing." Most parents love hearing that you care, that you don't know what to say, or that you are thinking of them and their child.

6. ***Avoid open ended questions***—We tend to ask open ended questions without even thinking, because that is the way we are used to communicating. But this is different. Instead, ask specific questions. For instance, imagine how the question *How are you?* feels to a parent whose child has died. That question can cause so much stress for someone living this nightmare. The reaction most parents have to that question is, "How am I? I am in agony and want to kill myself, that is how I am," or "Do you really want to know how I am?" Instead, try saying something more specific and simple such as, "If you are up to it, tell me what you did today." Make it easier for them to connect with you and tell you as much or as little as they want.

7. ***You do the work to connect***—For instance, if you want to see your friend and do something for her, instead of asking her what she wants or needs, you can simply suggest doing what you think might be helpful, such as baking or offering

to run to the store or doing laundry. If you want to see them, instead of asking if it would be okay, try, "I'd like to come by this Wednesday at 7:00. Does that work for you?" They can easily say no if they are not up to it. But push on. YOU make the commitment first, and keep making it. They are in shock and trying to pick up the pieces of the life they used to have. It's a lifelong process.

8. ***Recognize that being uncomfortable is okay***— It's not easy to be with someone who is in the worst pain imaginable. Nothing about this is easy. Yet it's not even close to what the parent is feeling. So it's okay if you feel awkward or uncomfortable when with your friend. Those uncomfortable feelings are soon replaced with deep feelings of compassion and gratitude the more time you spend with your friend. Not only will you help them, but they will help you! And I've been told by specialists that your friend's suffering will not always be as intense as it is now. I believe that is true, especially as she receives the kind of love and support she needs.

9. ***Leave your busy life at the door***—Not being in touch with your friend for a length of time, and then letting her know that it was because you had been "so busy," is readily experienced as one of the greatest hurts. Think about it. What could you possibly be doing that makes you so busy that you can't contact your grieving friend for a minute or

send a thoughtful text or email message? They see through the excuses anyway. Instead, even though you might feel very busy, take that minute to touch in. It will be so appreciated.

10. ***Embrace your friend***—Embrace the new friendship you can have and are developing with your friend. She will never be the same person again. How can she be? Her child has died, and tragedy always changes everything. Instead of judging her or acting as if you know what she should or should not be doing, love her in every moment she is struggling to make sense of what has happened to her child and to her life, overlook the upsetting things she might say or do in the midst of her suffering, and know that, as you walk alongside her during her lifelong journey, she will become one of the most dear friends you have ever known. She was always your dear friend, and now you can grow as friends again together to an even deeper level of friendship. I know that is what I am going to do. I hope you will join me.

What a beautiful message and I am happy to have been able to share it with you. There is a passage from the Book of Hebrews that speaks about God "going the distance" to relate to us in our weak humanity.

Since we, God's children, are human beings, made of flesh and blood, He became flesh and blood, too, by being born in human form; for only as a human being could He die and in dying, break the power of the devil who had the power of death. Only in that way could He deliver those who through fear of death have been living all their lives as slaves to constant dread. Hebrews 2:14-15.

We then should be glad that God doesn't treat us the way others treat us and as we so often treat Him. No matter what you do, no matter where you go, no matter the depth of your grief, God will always love you!

"Having loved His own who were in the world, He loved them to the end." John 13:1.

CHAPTER 5

With every passing season

*To every thing there is a season,
and a time to every purpose under the Heaven...
a time to mourn and a time to dance.*

Ecclesiastes 3:1,4

It is true that each year that passes brings with it a new way of grieving, with it a new perspective on loss and how we handle it. The numbness of the first year has worn off and the reality of the loss is now exposed, and the knowledge that this really happened is starting to sink in. It's like waking up from a bad dream that you can't quite shake off. Time has been moving along and you can't imagine that the first year since the loss of your child has already passed. It's also a number sequence thing. Once one is over, there will only be two to look forward to, then three, then four and so on. We know that time cannot stand still, it hasn't stood still and we are now entering a new phase.

Some say that the second year is harder than the first and I have to agree. It's your wake-up call that time has passed by and the reality that *your child is not coming home* hits hard. This is a new transition into another whole new world, as unexpected things begin to happen. For example, this may be the time that you might finally find yourself ready to start cleaning out the closets and storing the items that once were a part of the everyday life of you and your child. As you handle each item delicately, you'll realize that those size 5 PJs are not going to be outgrown now, the shoes are never going to get any bigger, and the little dresses are just that, little.

There will be an emptiness that sets in with each passing day of the "what was going to be." No more firsts. No first dates, no graduation, no prom, no wedding, no child of their own, no family holidays spent gathering around the fireplace singing Christmas songs or sitting at the holiday buffet table together; no one to watch you grow old.

It's a changing of the seasons that brings sorrows from times past into the present. You will watch others going through their celebrations and a pit will form in your gut—an overwhelming desire to just run away.

You may feel like this mother as she describes her recent discovery:

Yesterday, I decided to take my little pink thumb somewhere it's never been—green. I planted Sweat Peas, orange and yellow Magnolias, trimmed up shrubs, potted lavender, daisies, and sweet basil.

To wake up on April 1st to all this new life growing in and around my house is a little symbolic to how I feel. I am not trying to get all earthy on everyone here, but for the past two weeks, I have been lifeless. I have been buried under the grief.

It has only been in the past week that I have slowly eased out of it. I made myself run every day last week. I truly believe that I must take care of my physical state.

I pulled out my Bible again, began praying full sentences versus the bare murmurs before. So today, April 1, I have come out on the other side of that grief-stricken wave. Just to be clear, coming out of a wave does not mean that I am in the clear, but I have learned there is a clear difference between grieving and being buried under your grief. There is a difference between you grieving and the grieving controlling you and your thoughts. So today, I am grieving...not grief struck. Written by Summer Beavers.

A change in the seasons of grief is what she was feeling and having to learn to deal with, as she was beginning to become aware of the newness surrounding her and listening to her heart and God as to how to process it all. And many more times we will feel this change occurring as we walk this journey. With every passing season, things will change. Our thoughts will start to take form and we will battle some days and breeze through others, but we will be aware of it all.

As written by Clara Hinton:

It takes a lot of courage to face grief head on and say, "Today I will recognize that you are a part of my life. Today I will wrestle with you. Today you will not rule over me. Today I will face my fear."

So much of grief is fear. Fear of the unknown journey ahead. Fear of not knowing how to handle those emotional reminders of loss. Fear of feeling so empty and alone. There is fear of beginning a journey that feels so new and different and completely wrong. When loss enters our lives, our world as we once knew it suddenly feels like we are on foreign soil. We don't know how to speak the language, and we don't want to learn. Yet, we know that we are now living in a new place in life and we must face the days ahead with a resolve to go on.

Hope seems to know just when to appear to give us the courage needed to make it through the hour. A stranger smiles and we know that person truly wants us to feel some connection. The billowy clouds float without effort through the heavenly skies and remind us that God is watching over us. The birds begin chirping their Springtime song, and we know that our Winter season will soon change to Spring. The sun appears brighter than ever and warmth reaches all the way to the depths of our soul.

Chapter 5: With every passing season

Today is a brand new day, and you can grasp hold of some hope and defeat your fear. One day at a time. One step at a time. One thought at a time. You can make it! "Fear can be conquered when hope abides in the center of the heart."

There is another change occurring as well in that of our relationships. Some will have endured the changes along with us, but others will not. We will lose some old friendships for reasons we cannot understand but make new ones that I like to call *Divine Appointments*. God knows that not everyone can be a comfort to you during this all and so He wonderfully places others along our paths. These will be some of our new normal to deal with, and come to accept. Some will fall away for selfish reasons, others out of fear of saying the wrong thing or perhaps saying something that makes you cry, and they will not understand that it's okay, but instead leave a trail of dust from our doorsteps. We can't possibly expect those that have not been through what we are going through to understand all that goes along with it. We are carrying all this *"stuff"* and they cannot comprehend the concept of what that stuff is. They hurt for us and are sympathetic, and certainly care, but they get to go home to their families while you have to continue daily to work it out. They just don't get it. And we don't want them to either. So sadly, we will see changes in our relationships because we have had a child pass away.

As written by my dear friend and author, Susan Duke, in her book "Grieving Forward," she says this passage in one of her Chapters that stands out to me in a very strong way and that I knew I had to share with you. In her words:

A soft rain was falling one morning as I slipped from beneath my blankets and tiptoed to the window. The steady sounds of the raindrops reminded me of the new rhythm I was beginning to feel within my soul—the rhythm of life. As the fresh rain splashed gently against the windowpane, I thought of the countless tears that had also splashed upon the window of my soul to wash away the dust collected from the long season of grief.

Susan had lost her son, Thomas, in a tragic car accident in October of 1990. So she is no stranger to pain or loss. We mothers, who have lost a child, seem to have a silent understanding that there are no guarantees in this life and that bad things will and do happen. We just never expected it to happen to us. There is an almost and undeniable recognition when looking into the eyes of another woman who knows this type of loss. Nothing needs to be said, just a hug and a prayer that she will be okay.

We know our seasons of change will be challenging, heartbreaking, overwhelming, depressing and unbearable, but we also know that at some point, the grace and peace of God, the peace that surpasses all understanding will step in and our burden begins to lighten. God will be an ever present figure in this new life and as the days become weeks, months then years, we will be ever changing as the seasons; each one bringing with it a new outlook, a new memory and a new way of living. We at some place along the way realize that we have a purpose and that we are surviving. We can be strong in our faith and still fall to our knees knowing He is always right there to pick us up and carry us to the next place. He will hold us when we are starting to fall, He will carry us when we cannot take another step and He will love us as no other.

Joy does come again, God reminds us with this scripture:

Hear, O LORD, and be merciful to me; O LORD, be my help. You turned my wailing into dancing; you removed my sackcloth and clothed me with joy, that my heart may sing to you and not be silent. O LORD my God, I will give you thanks forever. Psalm 30:10-12.

God wants us to have joy back in our hearts again. He reminds us in *Ecclesiastes 3:1-11;*

There is a time for everything, and a season for every activity under Heaven: a time to be born and a time to die, a time to plant and a time to uproot, a time to kill and a time to heal, a time to tear down and a time to build, a time to weep and a time to laugh, a time to mourn and a time to dance, a time to scatter stones and a time to gather them, a time to embrace and a time to refrain, a time to search and a time to give up, a time to keep and a time to throw away, a time to tear and a time to mend, a time to be silent and a time to speak, a time to love and a time to hate, a time for war and a time for peace. What does the worker gain from his toil? I have seen the burden God has laid on men. He has made everything beautiful in its time. He has also set eternity in the hearts of men; yet they cannot fathom what God has done from beginning to end.

God knows there is a time for everything under Heaven and on earth. We cannot question His will. One day we will stand before Him and all will be revealed, but in His timing, not ours. Our changing begs of us to cry out for answers now, but we must trust Him. Have patience and endure this changing of seasons until we, too, are reunited unto Him and our loved ones.

I would like to think that when we get there, none of this will really matter anymore, but I am hoping that the Lord will set me down and explain the reasons, and then as scripture says, *"He will wipe every tear from their eyes. There will be no more death or mourning or crying or pain, for the old order of things has passed away." Revelation 21:4.*

Chapter 5: With every passing season

As shared by Carol Brown, a dear friend who lost her daughter, Jackie, 16 years ago in a motor vehicle accident, she brought up the topic of "goals." And it really touched a lot of other mothers;

I am thinking today about goals. Seems like an unlikely topic for this group, but I though I'd share anyway. When our grief is new and fresh it seems like we have only one goal...to rid ourselves of the constant searing pain that seems to be our unwanted companion 24/7. If only we could have a respite for just a little while! But the pain claws at us at all hours of the day and night, robbing us of any joy or purpose in life. But what if we intentionally and willfully changed that goal? What if we started to focus on something else other than the pain? Athletes often go onto the field with throbbing knees and aching backs because they are focused on winning the game. That is their goal. The desire to win is more important than anything else, and they accept the pain as a part of that process. What if we changed our focus to say...gratitude; gratitude for the life of the child God gave us, even if only for a little while. What if we started daily actively looking for God's hand of mercy and provision and determine to share what we find with others? And what if we started to reach out to people who need encouragement and strength? I'll bet you could think of other worthy goals for which to strive as well, even in the midst of your pain. And I think that this changing of focus may have an unintended consequence in that you will find that the pain is lessened and your joy, little by little, is returned.

In our seasons of change we do need to refocus and take to heart that we have some control over how we will determine our outcome. If we reach out to those who will listen, spend time with those who understand, albeit different circumstances and situations; still, surrounding yourself with life throughout your journey, you will set yourself up for a greater reward in the end, and with what God has yet to show you.

Not only so, but we also glory in our sufferings, because we know that suffering produces perseverance; perseverance, character; and character, hope. And hope does not put us to shame, because God's love has been poured out into our hearts through the Holy Spirit, who has been given to us. Romans 5:3-5.

...and teaching them to obey everything I have commanded you. And surely I am with you always, to the very end of the age. Matthew 28:20.

CHAPTER 6

He walks with me as the journey continues

Never will I leave you; never will I forsake you
Hebrews 13:5

God is an ever present part of our daily lives. He cares for us and walks this journey with us every second of every day. He will never turn away from us. He knows our path is a difficult one, He understands our pain. He watched His only son Jesus, be nailed to a cross to die as a part of the great plan for us to be reunited unto the father. He knows grief, sorrow and pain. So much, that when Jesus was on the cross at that very last moment, He could not even bear to look, and Jesus felt the fathers' presence leave him for that moment. God was not abandoning Christ but turning away from looking upon sin. The sins Christ bore for all of us. God knew that in an instant, Jesus was to be reunited at His right hand at the Throne of Grace as the great victor! Having fulfilled the purpose set before him.

1 Peter 2:24 says, "He himself bore our sins in his body on the tree, so that we might die to sins and live for righteousness; by his wounds, you have been healed."

We, too, may feel God has in some way turned away for a moment when we lose our child or loved one. We question, *"Where were you God when I needed you most?"* Remember, it is never Him that turns away, but us. He was with our child when they were received. We want answers though. We want to know why our child? What did we do so terribly wrong to deserve such punishment that instead of us, our child is gone? But our God is not a God of thieves, who would come and rob us of our most prized possessions. He is a God of love and compassion. He knew the day and the hour, the very moment that this would happen and He only asks that you trust Him that our children had fulfilled their purpose and it was just their time to go home. He did not *take* your loved one, but *received* them. After all, we all belong to Him first.

That is unacceptable to some. What purpose could an infant have had before they were even born, or what purpose did a sick child have that deserved such an end? Or to the one who passed in a car crash, a drowning, fire or murder?

Be reminded again of these two scriptures: *"Every day of my life was recorded in your book. Every moment was laid out before a single day had passed." Psalm 139:16.*

Chapter 6: He walks with me as the journey continues

"To be absent from the body is to be present with the Lord." 2 Corinthians 5:8.

No matter what the cause of death, we can find truth and confidence in His word. He has laid out the scriptures before us, and how can you know this? In *Hebrews 6:18,* it clearly states; *"It is impossible for God to lie."*

There are definitely times when I have to yell out to God, *"Hello? Can you hear me? I need you Lord, why can't I find you?"* Then I have to remember that He hears me, He's with me, but it's all about what is in His timing. First, what am I asking for Him to do for me? Am I being thankful for His love this day? Am I praising Him or is it just me being needy? I have learned that if I wake up each morning and say a simple prayer, *"Thank you, God, for this day. No matter what comes my way, happy or sad, good or bad, I know that you are right here in it with me."* That makes my day seem a lot lighter and more organized. And I am more likely to not be screaming out for Him but singing praises to Him.

He wants to hear from us about everything...not just hear our complaints or the typical "I need this or that, so can you give it to me Lord?" Why does it seem that when everything is going wrong, we cry out, "Lord, help me" but when things are going well, we forget to even say good morning to Him? Seems rather one sided to me. He listens for us every second of the day, but we only want Him when something's all messed up!

Another special mother, Shayla Moses, shared a precious and memorable moment with me after reading my first book, *"A Hole in My Heart ~ Finding Peace in God's Special Place."* I was quite touched after I read the following message below. She told me she had held this secret story in for a long time for fear of what others would think and of how it made her feel, but now felt she had to reveal it to all. It was a moment where she cried out to the Lord, and He answered in a way she never expected. In her own words, she wrote this to me;

I feel like I have to tell you this story. I read your book front to back last night and it was wonderful. I went to bed last night feeling very encouraged and uplifted, but also knowing that I have a lot of work to do on myself and my relationship with God so that I can get to a good place with my grief. There was a part in your book that gave me goose bumps and really hit home. I have only told this story to two people, and feel like I need to tell you because of the way this part of the book struck me. I think I don't tell this story because I can't get it out of my mouth without shaking and crying uncontrollably and because I feel like some people won't understand or may think I am crazy. Here goes...the part of your book I am talking about is when you were looking up at the stars and imagining God speaking to you about hope and saying "See how much I give you? Don't you know how much I love you?"

About two years after Jayce passed, I was having a REALLY tough night. I was deep down in the pits of grief and decided to go for a drive. I didn't want to upset my husband and little boy with my negative attitude—or with seeing me cry uncontrollably. I knew a big cry was coming, so out the door I went. I had only been gone about 15 minutes and my sadness was turning to anger in my car. Right after Jayce's death, I was extremely close with God. I prayed all day every day, keeping a constant conversation going and was comforted so much. I stopped doing that and now I was questioning God and yelling/ thinking "why would God do this to me and my little boy?" If God loved me so much, why would he put this on me? I was thinking I can't live with this...I can't do this. God must really be punishing me, but for what, I don't know. After screaming for a minute, I felt better and apologized to God, but I knew I was not okay and wasn't really sorry at the time. I meant what I said at the time, but wanted to apologize so I didn't get in "trouble" with God.

I got REALLY thirsty, so I turned around to go to the gas station and grab a Dr. Pepper. I wiped my eyes, took some deep breaths (so I didn't look like a crazy woman walking into this store) and went in. There was a lady at the counter watching me from the time I walked in the door and as I went back to the coolers.

I kept looking at her thinking I knew her (like I knew her well), but couldn't place her. I didn't want to go to the counter looking like this and it be someone I know, so I lingered at the cooler for a minute trying to place her so I could explain my appearance a little because I was sure I would be asked if I was okay. I just couldn't place her, so I took a deep breath and went to the counter. I paid for my drink and before I turned to walk out, she said, "Can you come outside with me for a minute? I have something to show you." Part of me was scared thinking I don't want to be killed or something, but part of me felt comfortable with her (I thought I knew her from somewhere). So, I just said, "I guess. I am going that way anyway"... and I am in a lit parking lot.☺

We walked to the middle of the parking lot, and she put her hand on my shoulder, pointed to the sky, and said, "Look. Tell me what you see." So, I did but I didn't see anything but a black sky and the moon. I was thinking; what is this lady doing? Is she crazy? I hope no one sees me looking at the sky with the gas station attendant. She then said, "Look harder, what do you see? I said "the moon." She said "Isn't it so beautiful?" I looked at it with her and she was describing the perfect colors blending in with the sky and everything about the moon that looked beautiful that night. Then she said, "Why would God give you such a beautiful sight tonight, if he wanted to hurt you? Would a God that doesn't love you give you this

Chapter 6: He walks with me as the journey continues

gift?" I didn't know what to think. Here I was just getting over screaming at God in my car and this lady is doing this! I just stood there looking at the moon and trying not to fall to my knees and cry in front of this woman. I felt her hand leave my shoulder right as that rush of tears came to me because I knew God loved me and I was taking my grief out on him. I turned to ask her how she knew me before she went back in, but she wasn't there. I figured she had to know me to know what I was going through and to say something like that to me.

I started walking back to the store and there was a man behind the register. I didn't see the woman anywhere. I didn't go in, but I thought she had to be here somewhere hiding or something because she didn't have long enough to walk back into the store. I didn't see her! I walked back to my car still looking around for her and noticed a bright yellow card on the ground by my car door with a smiley face on it. I picked it up and turned it over to see what it was. It said, "Smile! Jesus loves you." It didn't have a church name, phone number, email...nothing. Just a smiley face and a note from Jesus!

I drove home trying to process what just happened. I walked in the door and my husband said, "What's wrong? Are you okay? You look like something's wrong." I handed him the card and said, "Is that real? Does that card say what I think it says?" It did, so I told him the story right then and there. We cried together and kinda laughed about it and I tucked my little secret away.

I told my sister one night a few years later and we both cried (it took about 1.5 hrs to tell my sister because I couldn't stop hysterically crying). I can't explain that night or who that woman was. The story sounds crazy, but that's what happened and I think she was an angel that saved my life that night. I don't think I would have ever hurt myself, but I felt a very bitter cloud coming over me. I felt the feelings we all feel in dealing with this. But, that kind of snapped me out of it and I think about it quite a bit.

Knowing that others will now hear what a special experience I was given makes me feel wonderful. I think it is a remarkable story that people need to hear (and God probably did intend for others to hear), but I just have such a hard time saying it. I totally did not expect to read those lines in your book that shook me to the core because it was so close to my own experience.

Don't you just love that message? God does indeed use his angels to guide and remind us of His awesomeness! Shayla was headed in a dark place, angry with God but reaching out at the same time. She felt guilt for being angry with Him but justified her feelings because her son had died and her world was falling apart. Now she can be thankful for that moment when He did hear her crying out and sent

Chapter 6: He walks with me as the journey continues

a her a special messenger to help her…notice the woman who was pointing all these things out to her did not do anything more than comfort her with a gentle touch and words to remind her of God's greatness and His love for her? That is truly amazing to me, but that is the God we serve. He does love us, even when we are angry and yelling at Him. He will always find a way to reach us. I have no doubt that she is grateful now for that evening, and that it brought her heart back into a relationship with God in a positive way. I think we all need to be more thankful for the little reminders that He gives us.

I have personally made it a point to be more thankful. The attitude of gratitude that I mentioned earlier on, after all, was something He created us for a relationship with him, and He deserves our attention and affection. He walks with me and you everyday, no matter where we go. Though people in life will leave us or abandon us, He never does. When we wonder where He is at, all we need to remember is that He is always there and that all we need to do is turn around. He will find a way to reach us where we are. So, turn around and say hello to your Heavenly Father.

Anger is also an ever present part of our daily life and shows its ugly self in many different ways, so it's no shock that we would not find it to be included in some areas of our walk with God. As Christians, we fear being angry with Him, but listen up! He is much bigger than our anger and He can handle it. Some have, in their anger, questioned, "is there even such a person as God; because if there was, He would never have allowed this to happen"…but I say Hallelujah! Because if you are angry, then you have more faith than you realize for how can you be mad at someone or something you don't even believe in? Ahhh…got you on that one didn't I? But it's the truth. We can blame Him because we can't physically see Him and that makes it okay in some odd way to us… but that's just not how it works. He is a God who loves us.

But you, O Lord, are a compassionate and gracious God, slow to anger, abounding in love and faithfulness. Psalm 86:15.

I would like to share a wonderful story that was shared by my dear friend, Carol Brown, at our 2011 women's retreat we host annually called, "A Healing Journey." It is a story well worth the read!

Through the Fog into God's Masterpiece by Carol Brown

Last October, my husband and I decided to take a trip to Branson, Missouri. We also decided to end the trip with a couple of days in Petit Jean State Park in Mena, Arkansas. I was excited to make reservations at the Queen Wilhemena Lodge because I had heard such great things about it, and the view from the top of the mountain on which it was located.

Chapter 6: He walks with me as the journey continues

The weather was not good when we left Branson, and unfortunately, it only got worse as we made our way into Arkansas. When we began our assent up the mountain, we found ourselves surrounded by thick fog. The higher we climbed, the worse the visibility, until we were only able to see a short distance in front of us. Since there was no turning back, we slowly inched forward, following the dim glow of our car's headlights. As we strained our eyes to follow the road, we noticed that there seemed to be no guard rails on the side of the mountain, and I became rather worried about tumbling right off the side! Thankfully, there were mile markers along the way, telling us that we really were making progress, although it seemed we were totally lost in this ghostly, shrouded world.

We found ourselves in totally uncharted territory for we had not been this way before, and it was unsettling to say the least. At long last, I was able to see a parking lot up ahead, and as I looked to my left, there was the Queen Wilhemena Lodge, rising out of the fog. We had made it through "many dangers, toils, and snares" to our final destination!

The journey of grief is much like our experience in Arkansas. At the beginning, we feel shrouded in a fog of shock disbelief, and pain as we attempt to make our way up a road we have never before traveled. We try to follow the light of our faith, but that light which normally shines so brightly seems to have dimmed as we strain to look ahead into the future. In addition, we may experience fear that we will fall off the cliff of despair and sorrow. We can't seem to spot the mile markers that might give us some encouragement until we are right upon them. But those markers are meant to let us know we are headed in the right direction.

One day we wake up and our child's death is not the first thing we think of, or the last thing before falling asleep at night. Perhaps we enjoy an outing with a friend and are able to have a conversation that does not revolve around our loss. Or the time comes when we can take a trip with our husband or family and not feel guilty about having a great time. All these are markers along our journey to let us know we are nearing our destination.

Our destination as grieving moms is a place of healing and wholeness. The terms "healing" and "wholeness" do not infer that when we arrive, we will be exactly the same as we were before our child died. How can we be when an earthquake of loss and devastation has shaken us to our very foundations? Instead, we find that we have established a "new normal" and acceptance of the way things are, not the way we wish them to be. Our loss no longer defines us, but is simply another piece of the mosaic pattern that shapes and molds us into that beautiful work of art God has always intended us to become. The wound is cured, but the scar remains until we are together again with Jesus and our children.

In my church, we are blessed to have three pieces of stained glass in the windows. These pieces were given in memory of two young people in the same family who had passed away. I have spent much time contemplating these windows. I have noticed the different patterns and colors, some dark, some light, some bright white. When the sun shines through them just so, shafts of pure light mix with these colors to form dazzling patterns on the floor. To me, it is a picture of life. Some of the pieces are dark and sorrowful, some tinted with joy and laughter, some bright white with the awesome touch of the Master Craftsman. As He carefully and lovingly places each piece, a beautiful, reverent picture begins to take shape. Only when we stand before Him will our picture finally be complete, the Father's light shining through us, lighting us up with His undying love. Then the picture will make perfect sense.

Until then, my sisters, take heart. You are not alone, and burdens shared are burdens lightened. We are fellow travelers headed toward the same destination, and we will get there! If we keep patiently walking toward the light we have, dim though it may seem at times, we will draw closer to journey's end each day until we finally arrive to find joy and purpose waiting for us.

To me, that was such a perfect description and analogy of our loss. We are simply in a fog, but God can see through it all and He will reveal all to you when you are seeing with spiritual eyes and not those rose colored glasses we try to hide behind pretending everything in the world is okay with us, while cringing on the inside with our emotions. You have to take the blinders off and see all that is still around you. He has given you much to appreciate, so take hold of it. Take hold of Him and find peace and joy again!

CHAPTER 7
I DO have favor with God

By this I know that thou favourest me,
because mine enemy doth not triumph over me.

Psalm 41:11

We all have our moments and times where nothing seems right or real anymore. It has been six years since Robert went home and I miss him so much... but yet I know how deeply he suffered here and that he is completely whole now. I also have the promise that I will see him again. Life is short, messy and down right difficult but it's only temporary. We have so much joy to come, and I know we are going to be okay. We have had precious favor with God to have been chosen by Him personally to have such amazing children to begin with so I trust Him for what is promised to come!

I love the scripture, *John 14:1-3*, so much that I include it on every book I sign. What this verse tells us is this;

"Do not let your hearts be troubled. You believe in God; believe also in me. My Father's house has many rooms; if that were not so, would I have told

you that I am going there to prepare a place for you? And if I go and prepare a place for you, I will come back and take you to be with me that you also may be where I am."

I went through a weird stage here a few months back, questioning God's favor in my life and it really got me deeply discouraged. Then as I was reading in a book someone gave me of the Psalms; mind you it had been sitting there for over two months, I picked it up and started to read. At that moment, I noticed on TV that Joel Osteen had come on. Now I have to admit, I am not much of a TV preacher person, but as I was reading, I left it on and I heard him say something that changed my depression that day. He started talking about having favor with God, and what I believe he called the little Moses fish. He said that the shark opens its mouth to devour the fish and the little fish emits a toxin that paralyses the shark's mouth for a few minutes and the little fish gets away. The shark leaves in a panic and all is good for this preyed upon fish—it gets away safely. God has favor with this little fish to protect it, and…HE HAS FAVOR WITH US! It's called JESUS! When the enemy (for us Satan) starts to clamp down on us, we have our protection force to get away. I loved that analogy and its truth and how it changed my life that day.

Depression is such a terrible thing and it drives us away from God. But we must remember that it is us who turns and not God. He is faithful, always.

I know we will find the truth in His word because we have favor with Him. It's hard to be a ministry leader and be grieving ourselves; it gets draining at times, and it's only natural that one would feel this way. I know that in those moments, I just need to trust that God is already working this all out for me. I cannot let the enemy come in and steal my favor with God and you should not either. Don't let the enemy win! Claim your favor with God. He desires to give it to you.

Think again of Nehemiah rebuilding the wall, the story of David and Goliath, Job, King David, Ruth, Abraham and Moses; all of the ones we read about that had favor with God mentioned in His book. If God then, could show favor to even one of these recorded about in the Bible, then why not to us? We seem to want to believe that God only showed favor to those in Biblical times and not to us who are in the here and now. He shows it everyday. The first spaceship that landed on the moon, the child who was in an orphanage and now has a home and family, the rebuilding of entire neighborhoods and cities after natural disasters strike, the outpouring of love for those affected by 9-11, and so many more "favors" God has shown. The list is endless. It was not only those mentioned in the Bible that had God's favor upon them, it is us, too! Perhaps some have more favor than others you say? Wrong! We all have favor with Him. Are you claiming it and receiving it? Are you being obedient to Him and walking with Him? We must seek it and claim it, and He will bless us when we do.

Sometimes our favor seems lessened or dim, to that I would reply something profound that I read on a friends blog;

"At times our own light goes out and is rekindled by a spark from another person. Each of us has the cause to thank with deep gratitude of those who have re-lit the flame within us." (Anonymous Quote).

Throughout your life, you will need this capacity to believe in yourself, in your friends, in your talents and in your family. You'll also need to believe in things you can't measure or even hold in your hand. Here, I am talking about love, about Jesus, that great power that will light your life from the inside out, even during its darkest, coldest moments. (Summer Beavers).

To me, she is speaking of the favor we have with God who brings others into our lives to fulfill greatness, to see the light of His love.

"It's not how long a star shines, what is remembered is the brightness of the light." (Anonymous Quote).

Do you ever notice a bright full moon? One that is so bright it is almost blinding and hard to focus on? There is something so peaceful, so calming and so alluring looking into a full moon. The misty

Chapter 7: I DO have favor with God

shadow that encircles it, somehow always makes me feel closer to God. It is as if you can see the whole universe on a clear night, while gazing into the star-filled night sky. To me, there is nothing more beautiful about the night than to see this magnificent sight. Therefore, I know there has to more than this and I tell Him that every night while studying the night sky. God is up there. Yes, He is in it. He has shown favor in it and in me for giving me the sight to see it.

I found myself recently questioning His favor, though and it came about in how I was handling my grieving, and so I reached out to a friend for some advice. I told her that I was lying in bed the night before, unable to sleep and wrestling with how I was grieving my son's death. I told her I could not understand why He had chosen me for this ministry and all the blessings that come from it, because I had this absurd question that I did not know how to ask if I believed I had favor with Him. You see, there was one area I was not reconciled with and so I asked her, "Why don't I grieve like some of our moms?" Is it because I am dulled of my loss or in some bizarre way over it? I just don't feel the need to dwell on his death...is that normal? Or do you think that because he was so sick and I now know his suffering is over, that this in some way dismissed my loss in my mind (not my heart but my mind)? He had been diagnosed critically ill from two months of age and his prognosis was that he would likely pass by 10 years of age. I told her I felt the word I thought I was searching for was more of one of concern.

She gently replied this to me, *"Autumn, everyone's path is different. When we change our focus from the pain to other things like reaching out to others, we find that the pain is somehow lessened. Some of the moms may find themselves stuck in the grief journey, unable to move forward due to resentment, guilt, anger, or even self pity. You are at the point of moving on and that is a good, healthy thing. You will never forget your son, as if you could in a million years! But instead of being a source of pain, he has become a source of your outreach ministry to other moms. So don't feel guilty. Your recovery should be a source of encouragement to others who are just beginning on this journey. This is God showing favor on you!"*

Wow, that really hit home and surely answered my question. I decided it was okay then, that God has shown favor for reasons that were within my obedience to serve Him and ultimately others. So, I am not abnormal because I walk a little differently than others. We all grieve differently anyway. There are no set rules for this. I know that God has been filling up that hole in my heart by reaching out because this ministry is my passion; but God has become even more of a passion to me lately, if that makes sense? I am absorbed in wanting to please

Him and it makes me feel good to help others! Perhaps that is a blessing of favor He has shown and who am I to question His gift to me? I now see that Glory revealed as He is using me just the way I am.

> *Remember me with favor, my God,*
> *for all I have done for these people.*
>
> *Nehemiah 5:19*

Ministry for me has been a very healing journey. I find myself feeling joy in reaching out to another in their time of need. I am known for putting my own grief on the back burner to run to the aide of another who is crushed in spirit and help lift them back up. I am by no means a miracle worker, but I get such a wonderful, warm feeling in being there for someone else. I don't ask for anything in return, never even really thought about that until just now, but I honestly have no expectations of receiving anything back at all.

I serve our God through ministering to others who are walking in these same old grief shoes, wearing out our soles and souls…if that makes sense. If you are a bereaved parent, it will resonate within you. But to help another is a humbling way of serving our Father and is most healing for us. Not everyone can do this kind of 'work' on a daily basis, and I have to admit that it gets draining and overwhelming—even a little depressing at times. It also leaves little time for me to reflect on my own loss, but it is who God called me to be, and so I just do it!

I am not anyone, in my eyes, extra special. I have no real education in ministry, but I have had a seed planted and watered by my own tears and that of other grieving mothers, and I have learned that we ALL need each other. We cannot walk this alone. It is too much for one to individually bear without having others to lean on who understand. God knew I could not do this alone by any means, so He sent me special "others" who serve and help with the tasks laid out before us. These special helpers sense and know when the burden is weighing too heavily on me and He sends them at lightning speed to assist me. I am so grateful for those He has put onto my path…more than mere words can say.

I often wonder how others that we read of in the Bible stories felt with ministering to others. Did they question God for the gift He gave them also? Jesus made the ultimate sacrifice, but before he returned to Heaven, he taught! He spoke kind words of encouragement to his disciples and followers. He told us that the path to righteousness is narrow and that only few would enter, it would be hard and the load heavy. But He also told us that He would carry our burden and lighten our load;

"For My yoke is easy and My burden is light."
Matthew 11:30

Chapter 7: I DO have favor with God

And so we are also reminded this:

> *Watch your thoughts; they become words.*
> *Watch your words; they become actions.*
> *Watch your actions; they become habits.*
> *Watch your habits; they become character.*
> *Watch your character; it becomes your destiny.*
>
> *Author Unknown*

That is a good lesson to follow. We must be watchful of many things. Yes, He will carry us, but we must be committed with a whole heart and He knows the heart and what lies within it. We cannot hide anything from Him. He knows the reasons we even do the things we do, the thoughts we have and the outcome of our destiny.

Because He has favor upon us, He watches over us. And that means everything to me and it should to you, too!

*" We are all here to be of service
to one another...to grace one another's lives
with offerings of our skills and talents,*

*Our time and energy,
our resources, and our love..."*

~ Caroline Joy Adams ~

Photograph by Autumn Ater

CHAPTER 8
All good deeds

*Praise be to the God and Father
of our Lord Jesus Christ, the Father
of compassion and the God of all comfort,
who comforts us in all our troubles,
so that we can comfort those in any trouble
with the comfort we ourselves have received
from God. For just as the sufferings of Christ
flow over into our lives, so also
through Christ our comfort overflows.*

2 Corinthians 1:3-5

This Chapter has a special *twist* to it. I wanted to share with you some of the wonderful deeds others have done that has helped many along this path. Some of these people who you will read about will have lost a child and some, thankfully, have never lost a child, but who have been affected by loss and have reached out and are doing some really incredible things. Some just have enormous words of wisdom to share and that alone will bless you. At the end of this Chapter, I will be sharing some photographs with you of those throughout this book and its Chapters, so you can meet these precious angels!

My first story starts out with my childhood friend Diane (Strong) Barstow; she has two children, a boy and a girl. Her 12 year old daughter, ReAnna, is a Girl Scout, in the schools gifted and talented program, and does a lot of community work. For example, she works with senior citizens and also provides a very special gift of helping maintain a garden for children that have passed, called Children's Memorial Garden, located in Toms River, New Jersey, so parents have a place to go to pray and reflect.

Since the 4th Grade, she has been a member of the "Impac Group" that is involved in the care of the gardens. The children have witnessed parents, siblings, grandparents and others, coming to reflect and pour out their hearts. ReAnna has come home crying from there so many times after watching parents leave gifts, statues and flowers.

It is emotional and has been hard on these children who all want to help maintain the gardens... but still they want to make the place beautiful and comforting for those visiting. This is something that will make ReAnna (and the other members) more compassionate people. For ReAnna though, she has learned that she is letting a piece of their lives touch hers. How very precious! At such a young tender age, she is learning to leave her mark—her "good deed."

Chapter 8: All good deeds

Diane's son, James, age 19, has also done some amazing things as well, including becoming an Eagle Scout at the age of 17 and is involved in many community projects. In Diane's words, "I am very proud that he has left his mark as well and has been given deserved recognition from many world leaders". What mother would not be proud of two such amazing, passionate children? Good deeds taught by good parents to receptive children. Now that's truly a gift and blessing in itself.

Next, there is my dear friend, Dianne Cronan Fleming, who donates her time to make beautiful photo graphics for our moms and always has a compassionate word for others, being no stranger to knowing loss herself after her son, Scotty, passed in 2009. She devotes endless hours to showing compassion and empathy to others with beautiful prayers and acknowledging the others' losses. As I was reading her Facebook Memorial Blog about her son, Scotty, I saw this incredibly cute message posted by a longtime friend, Lynda Lamb, whom she met as a "military brat" in her own words, while their parents were on base at Yokota AFB, Japan.

"You are like a one legged duck (I mean this with love, and only love) ... sailing across the water so smooth to look at, but paddling like heck under the water ... where no one can see

... KEEP PADDLING!"

Isn't that what all of us bereaved moms feel like...a wounded one legged duck? But instead of going round and round in circles, we are as Linda puts it, paddling like heck under water (through the stress of our loss). Well said, girlfriend!

Dianne knows how good it makes her feel inside to know that she is blessing someone's day, even if by a comment, a prayer or photo graphic. This really helped her to hear because sometimes in her own prayers, even as of very recently, she asked God if there was anything she might have said or done in His name for the sake of others that might have been taken in vain. Linda's comment let her know that God hears her prayers and gives her the answers through friendships with others. No good deed left undone where God is concerned.

I cannot forget to share with you my dear friend, Marcia Poe-Hulsey. What a woman of God we find here. She spends literally hours of each day making the most beautiful graphics for our online Facebook Group. She tells me she actually feels a connection to each child and their mother. She weeps many tears in doing this work, a ministry in itself. She asks for nothing in return as it brings her great joy to put a smile on another grieving mom's face. You see, Marcia's daughter, Lorena, passed in July of 2008 from a Hypertrophic Cardiomyopathy. She was only 31 years old. Yet, with all of Marcia's grief, she still finds time to reach out and embrace another mother who is hurting. I honestly cannot thank her enough for what she does for *A Hole in My Heart* and these precious women. She is a rare diamond in the rough…a sparkling joy to the heart!

My dear friend, Karen Adkins, has been going through a terrible turmoil since the death of her son, Luis, in 2008 from a tragic motor vehicle wreck. Luis was a young man, who was headed down the wrong path once and his poor choices caught up with him. He one day found himself landed in a jail cell and had time to reflect on his choices and behaviors. A clerical error prevented him being transferred from one County to another and in that moment of opportunity, God sent a messenger to speak with some of the inmates. The preacher sat down with Luis and right there, after sharing all he did, he gave his life to Christ. Can you hear the angels rejoicing? I know this meant a lot to Karen, as she had a great love for the Lord and her son, of course, and a prayer seemed to be answered. He was sent the next day and served his time and released.

With a new perspective on life now and Christ living in his heart, he felt convicted and urged to help his friends. Regrettably, they were not listening and after a drunk driver got behind the wheel of a vehicle with three other passengers, one being Luis, speeding down a highway, the young man lost control of the vehicle and crashed. Three walked away, but Luis, who was the only one sober and seat-belted in, wasn't so fortunate. He was killed instantly as the car hit the embankment. One of the passengers in the rear of the car told everyone that he had spoken to Luis and that he indicated he was just fine…but paramedics and medical professionals said there was no way he ever spoke—he suffered severe blunt head trauma and was pronounced at the scene.

I remember talking to Karen the first time after her son had passed. She had called me after hearing about *A Hole in My Heart* and wanted some help. I instructed her to go to the book of Proverbs for some reason and she gasped. She stated that it had taken her a bit to go into Luis's room but when she did, his Bible was there beside his bed and marked with bookmark was the book of Proverbs. God was giving her some additional comfort in that as she knew it was his way of letting her know he really was okay. We shared a lot that evening through many tears and she stated that Luis had told her on many occasions after letting Christ into his heart that he was gonna find a way to help his friends. Perhaps now, through his death, he is finally reaching some of those that needed it most.

Karen and I recently talked and she shared with me that she had been a Christian for as long as she can remember but hadn't always acted like one. She stated, *"My heart is there but my actions speak differently sometimes. I think that's why I started getting depressed. I was turning from God too often and not making Him or His word a priority in my life. I haven't been very thankful lately and He needed me to hear your message on favor. So you and I both have favor with God, Autumn, and it doesn't matter how long you have been a Christian or might be the one that has back slid (Aka...ME) but we do have His favor...otherwise what would we have? The enemy; and that is someone I DO NOT NEED!"*

I told Karen she was right, we would have nothing. A life without God is no life, strictly my opinion! I know I back slide—I get bogged down when everything comes at me all at once!

We thanked God for recognizing that he knows the human in us, but yet He always has His ways of bringing us back to Him. We know that negativity only draws more negativity and who needs that? We all have our moments and we've both been down and now are coming back up the hill again, but we also know how easy it is to lose everything in the blink of an eye and so we must stay prepared. The only thing we can do is to stay in the Word and trust Him in our times of trouble, be confident because we do have favor with Him. "I never realized that until tonight's message," she also admitted. She thought she was a "*nobody*," but God says we are somebody and worthy; to Him anyway and that's got to be enough. Anyone else that finds us worthy is a bonus blessing!!!

> *"And we pray this in order that you may live*
> *a life worthy of the Lord and may please him*
> *in every way: bearing fruit in every good work,*
> *growing in the knowledge of God."*
>
> *Colossians 1:10*

About one year after Robert's death, we had our grandson, Vincent, spend the night. He was about three years old, and he was climbing up onto our queen size bed. After getting up there, he stopped bouncing and was looking into the corner of the bedroom ceiling. I looked up (thinking maybe he saw a spider or moth) but noticed nothing there. He then said "Hi Uncle Boo Boo." I just looked over at Scott and we both did a little pouty smile, but Vinny was persistent. He then said "Gramma, look! It's Uncle Boo Boo." I realized the urgency in his voice and looked up and again saw nothing but said to Vinny, "Do you see Uncle Robert?" and he seriously replied "Yes, he's smiling." I was now sure he was seeing something that Scott and I could not see, but he just kept looking there at that corner and then as quickly as the conversation started, he said, "Uncle Boo Boo's going bye-bye now but he'll be back Gramma." I was in shock I think and just said, "Bye Robert…see ya later alligator." Which were also the exact words I used at his graveside service when I kissed him for the last time and before Scott came up (as seen on our video) and kissed him and said the very same words. I remember the tears swelling up in my eyes and as I went to bring my hands together to wipe them away, I could smell Robert's scent on my hands. I had this happen before and now I knew I was not going crazy—Robert was there. It was just like a miracle and I know without a doubt that what Vinny saw was really there. He saw Robert! Perhaps children, before the age of accountability, can see things we cannot. I will never forget that day and how it made me feel. Another good deed well done and well received.

So what does the Bible say about doing good deeds? Let's review some key scriptures.

And whatever you do, in word or deed, do everything in the name of the Lord Jesus, giving thanks to God the Father through him. Colossians 3:17.

And let us consider how to stir up one another to love and good works. Hebrews 10:24.

For it is God who works in you, both to will and to work for his good pleasure. Philippians 2:13.

Show yourself in all respects to be a model of good works, and in your teaching, show integrity, dignity, and sound speech that cannot be condemned, so that an opponent may be put to shame, having nothing evil to say about us. Slaves are to be submissive to their own masters in everything; they are to be well-pleasing, not argumentative, Titus 2: 7-9.

But the anointing that you received from him abides in you, and you have no need that anyone should teach you. But as his anointing teaches you about everything, and is true, and is no lie—just as it has taught you, abide in him. 1 John 2:27.

And the most important one that stands out more than any other is this:

So in everything, do to others what you would have them do to you, for this sums up the Law and the Prophets. Matthew 7:12.

There are many more scriptures, but these stand out so vividly. God instructs us in many ways through His word and He only desires for us to follow His words by example. There are different good deeds done all the time—so many that I could not possibly list them all, but every one of us knows of a good deed someone has done for us and/or for others and that is doing the work of the Father. Christ calls us to love God first and love our neighbor as ourselves;

"Love the Lord your God with all your heart and with all your soul and with all your mind and with all your strength. The second is this: 'Love your neighbor as yourself.' There is no commandment greater than these." Mark 12:30-31.

This is then the greatest commandment…to love (Him and each other as He loves us.) There is no greater feeling than doing something to help someone

Chapter 8: All good deeds

else. It makes you feel good inside and it pleases the Father immensely. Remember here these beautiful words preached by Jesus himself in the Sermon on the Mount:

The Beatitudes

*"Blessed are the poor in spirit,
for theirs is the kingdom of Heaven.*

*Blessed are those who mourn,
for they will be comforted.*

*Blessed are the meek,
for they will inherit the earth.*

*Blessed are those who hunger
and thirst for righteousness,
for they will be filled.*

*Blessed are the merciful,
for they will be shown mercy.*

*Blessed are the pure in heart,
for they will see God.*

*Blessed are the peacemakers,
for they will be called children of God.*

*Blessed are those who are persecuted
because of righteousness,
for theirs is the kingdom of Heaven.*

> *Blessed are you when people insult you,*
> *persecute you and falsely say all kinds of evil*
> *against you because of me. Rejoice and be glad,*
> *because great is your reward in Heaven,*
> *for in the same way they persecuted the prophets*
> *who were before you."*
> *Matthew 5: 3-12*

God has laid out His instruction booklet for you, His love letter to you called The Holy Bible. It is up to you if you will follow its instruction as we are all given free will, but it is my sincerest hope that you will meditate on the above as you will find great truth, wisdom and knowledge in them. All good deeds are in His book…why not have a look?

For the LORD is good and his love endures forever;
his faithfulness continues through all generations

Psalm 100:5

Here are those photos I promised to share!

Carol Brown   Jackie Brown   Clara Hinton

Chapter 8: All good deeds

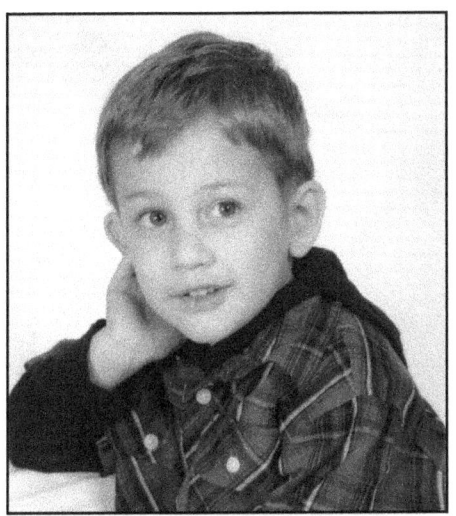

Vincent (my grandson) at age 3

Dianne Fleming

Scotty Fleming

Luis, Karen and Jerry Adkins

Susan Duke

Diana Barton &
Diane Cordova

Barbara Rice &
Diana Barton

Nancy Guthrie

Summer & Kelsie Beavers

Dewitt Jones

Kelsie Beavers

James, Diane, ReAnna & Tom Barstow

ReAnna Barstow

Chapter 8: All good deeds

Margaret Balian & her friend, Cathy

Marcia Poe Hulsey

Jayce Moses

Jayce & Shayla Moses

Dr. Alan Wolfelt

Gina & Kaylee Petner-Ramos

*Without purpose, passion, and a sense
that we are making a difference,
what meaning does our life really have,
and why should we strive to do our best work?
The beauty of appreciation is that
we can each give it to anyone we choose.*

*It costs nothing,
except a few moments of our time ~*

Anonymous

CHAPTER 9
Praises for His love

Love the LORD your God with all your heart
And with all your soul and with all your strength.

Deuteronomy 6:5

Praising God for His mighty works in our life is a wonderful thing to do each morning as you rise, throughout the day, and as you lay down for the evening. Life is full of joyful miracles every day and we sometimes overlook these precious gifts given by Him. He hears our thoughts, knows our heart and sees everything we do. We are either pleasing Him or disappointing Him, and we all fall short on that one. Yet, he continues to love us and never gives up on us. What an awesome God we serve!

I can't count how many times I have prayed to Him in times of doubt and troubles, and although I know He hears my pleas, I am reminded each time that somewhere along the way of my reaching out to Him, I forgot to praise Him. For no other reason than He is just who He is. That's a conflict we all, as Christians, struggle with. It's the very human in us. He is Spirit and we are carnal, and we cannot possibly see things the way He does. But I know we must be more focused on Him and thanking Him at every turn and every moment.

We all know that "someone" who likes to make us feel bad or guilty for not spending more time with God. Not reading enough of the word or going to church more often, praying less and the list goes on, but we are not called to judge others; that has been left to Christ. We just need to remind them that no one is perfect. We are flesh now, and yes the Spirit lives in us, but we fall short every day. All I can say is that when life throws its grubby dirt in your eyes... you just need to go wash them out so you can see more clearly. Only God can convict others and make them seek change. Yet some think it is their Christian duty to correct others. There is nothing wrong with speaking the Word to someone and gently guiding them if you see they are struggling, but criticism can also drive someone away. We must show others by example and that includes praising God for His great kindness to us.

As put into a wonderful quote here; *Nothing but Heaven itself is better than a friend who is really a friend. Plautus.*

I found this beautiful poem that I would like to share:

Heaven's Playground

There's a playground up in Heaven
Where all the children go;
It's a place that's full of laughter
Unlike this world here below.

There's a playground up in Heaven
Where all our angels play;
And the hearts there are so happy
Unlike our hearts feel today.

There's a garden up in Heaven
Where the roses blossom still;
While below it feels like winter
All the angels feel no chill.

In that garden up in Heaven
You will never find a tear;
How we wish we could be with them
Or we still had them down here.

There's no crying in that playground
Just their happy faces there;
There's no pain and there's no heartache
There's no illness or despair.

They're too busy with their playing
They're too happy making friends;
It's their parents wanting answers
And their broken hearts to mend.

As they play in Heaven's playground
All our little angels sing;
They don't question why they're up there
They don't ask for anything.

All our children play together
In that playground in the sky.

Author Unknown

I thought that was so very beautiful! You know, it still amazes me that it's been six years since Robert passed away and that with each year's passing, it truly has brought with it a different "feeling"…a completely different and new perspective. I can almost envision the little children and so many other children (all of our children) playing on the softest of green grass, tumbling on it with Jesus as he tickles them, their laughter bursts like little bubbles in the air around them as lions and lambs watch on and butterflies are everywhere! Almost makes me want to cry just writing that. But our Father is good to give us these little wishful insights into His kingdom. I find myself praising His Holy name in it all.

Spring is here, and everything is blooming. The fragrant scents are coming in through the windows, which by the way; in Texas, is a rarity as the weather here only gives you a small time frame for such "niceness" with the temperatures. With slightly warmer days and cooler nights, it is so breathtaking to

Chapter 9: Praises for His love

just feel the wind blowing through the sheer curtains, and it reminds me of days past, when I was a child playing outside, catching lightening bugs, and wearing culottes! And oh, those baby doll pajamas—they were something else. To have a pair of those made you a serious princess (insert childish giggling here). But those memories are also ones of innocence and when being carefree in it all was only natural and saying prayers was routine. I am remembering at bedtime, we always said the following, ever famous prayer;

"Now I lay me down to sleep, I pray the Lord my soul to keep, if I should die before I wake, I pray the Lord my soul to take."

Today, as a grown woman, I cannot remember the last time I said that prayer that way or wore "baby dolls" or even thought to buy something like them. But the point is, we grow up and become "mature" and our thoughts of God change…as do the seasons of life. And we need to remember that we are instructed to come before God as a little child…

> *"I tell you the truth;*
> *anyone who will not receive*
> *the kingdom of God like a little child*
> *will never enter it."*
>
> *Luke 18:17 and Mark 10:15*

The two scriptures listed above are identical in the NIV Bible. It is amazing how Jesus has instructed us not once, but twice that this is the only way to enter Heaven. We need to find our "child-self" and pray that we become innocent minded again as we once were. This is surely another way to praise our Heavenly Father. Be reminded of this scripture, as well, for it speaks such volumes of truth;

In I Thessalonians 4:13-18, we read: *Brothers and sisters, we do not want you to be uninformed about those who sleep in death, so that you do not grieve like the rest of mankind, who have no hope. For we believe that Jesus died and rose again and so we believe that God will bring with Jesus those who have fallen asleep in him. According to the Lord's word, we tell you that we who are still alive, who are left until the coming of the Lord, will certainly not precede those who have fallen asleep. For the Lord himself will come down from Heaven, with a loud command, with the voice of the archangel and with the trumpet call of God, and the dead in Christ will rise first. After that, we who are still alive and are left will be caught up together with them in the clouds to meet the Lord in the air. And so we will be with the Lord forever. Therefore encourage one another with these words.*

When you are fearful of death or the uncertainty of life, revel in this message:

> *"Where, O death, is your victory?*
> *Where, O death, is your sting?"*
>
> *1 Corinthians 15:55*

Chapter 9: Praises for His love

To me, this entire Chapter is like one big scripture of praises to God. How could we not meet the rising sun each day or the setting of it and not be in awe of His presence and might? Look out of your window each morning and whether you see bad weather or good, thank Him for the day itself and what joys and blessings it will bring. Though sorrow is a part of life, there is so much joy. Even when the joy seems distant because of a tragedy, God is holding on to you even tighter and asking you to see with your spiritual eyes that He loves you and will never leave you.

… "Stand up and praise the LORD your God, who is from everlasting to everlasting."

"Blessed be your glorious name, and may it be exalted above all blessing and praise. You alone are the LORD. You made the Heavens, even the highest Heavens, and all their starry host, the earth and all that is on it, the seas and all that is in them. You give life to everything, and the multitudes of Heaven worship you." Nehemiah 9:5-6.

Every time you see a butterfly, remember the new life… the new normal that God has given unto it. What once appeared to fade away and die now emerges into new life and is re-born into what we call "a butterfly." Have you ever seen anything more beautiful, graceful or majestic?

A butterfly came floating by,
I thought I knew its face,
It landed on my shoulder,
and spread its wings of lace.

I looked and saw it smiling,
as it winked and flew away,
I'm sure I heard it whisper,
"We'll meet again one day."

Author Unknown

My friend, Savannah, shared this beautiful vision with me a while back about a butterfly and I have never forgotten her words shared here:

Autumn, I had an amazing vision years ago about a butterfly landing on God's finger and I saw it kiss His finger. When God rose up His Hand high, I could see the butterfly hold so tight to God's finger that I thought its legs would snap. Then, He told the butterfly, 'Arise, for I've created you to fly.'

How I thank you, Savannah, for that beautiful photograph in my mind. Yes, He is creator of all things and worthy of our praises. No matter what has happened, even that of the death of our child or children. He received them safely home and is watching over them until we are reunited once again. A recent friend was struggling so bad to praise God in her recent loss, our conversation went something like this;

Chapter 9: Praises for His love

Barbara: I've been going to Bible study and went to church tonight. During the service, I asked God to come into my heart. I want to praise Him but it's hard. We will always have our moments but we will have God and each other to pull us through, right? I just can't wait for us all to be in eternal glory with the Lord and our angels. Still, Lord Jesus, just come!

Me: Believe me, as you get to know your Bible better, you will realize Jesus is coming faster than you think. 1,000 years here is but 1 day in Heaven. It will be as the blink before the blink before the blink of our eyes even thinking to blink that we will see them again. The truth is though; the ***hardest thing*** for a bereaved mom is in the *wanting* to go to Heaven for the right reasons. We have to want to go to be in HIS presence and with that in our hearts first, then we shall receive our reward of His gifts, ours being our children! Together for all eternity! Keep your eyes and heart focused on HIS kingdom first and all you desire will be given to you. You will see and be with your child again. He promises that to you. You gave Him your heart and He alone knows your heart and soul. It's hard when you feel you are going this journey alone, but you are not. Only you know how you truly feel as we all understand the motions of this type of grief, but you were the one in the relationship with your child and that love can NEVER die. Nothing on earth can separate you both from that. But it's His love that brought you together to begin with! So praise His name and do not give up the good fight.

It is hard to find yourself singing songs of praise when you suffer the loss of a child but God wants you to be trust Him. Be obedient and confident in His word. He will never fail you. The Psalms are so beautiful to read and sing of the many praises through turmoil David went through, including the loss of his son, but he never waivered. He never gave up on God. He trusted that no matter the situation, God was right there in it with him and would deliver him of his tormented heart and mind. And that very God is the God we still serve today, who is alive in us and will carry us through…always!

"For I will turn their mourning into joy, And I will comfort them, and give them joy for their sorrow."

Jeremiah 31:13

Photograph taken by Autumn Ater

CHAPTER 10
I have a purpose and a plan

For I know the plans I have for you," declares the LORD, "plans to prosper you and not to harm you, plans to give you hope and a future.

Jeremiah 29: 11

A friend recently shared with me how God is using me and my loss in an amazing way! She shared these words, "I can't imagine going through what you have been through, and coming out on the other side giving God the glory! He has truly blessed you!"

I could only reply that I just listened and was obedient to His calling of me to ministry, and that is so weird to me because I have not always been a very faithful person in the past, but He chose me anyway. It has made my relationship with Him closer, but I am just a baby still. Maybe that's the way He wants us to be to some extent though—that way we are always searching to learn more.

And I think we all feel like that way sometimes, too! Even though we are not always faithful to Him, He is always faithful to us, and we are so blessed for that. I look at it like this...we all have a purpose and we know GOD ALWAYS HAS A PURPOSE AND A PLAN. The question most people never ask is, "what is it Lord?" We tend to seek it from others and from somewhere within ourselves, when we need to be asking Him. That's what I was doing in prayer when He planted the seed for *A Hole in My Heart Ministry*. I never questioned Him or His purpose, as I might have if another human would have said or suggested, "Hey, Autumn, I think you should start a support group for bereaved moms".... seems strange maybe but its the truth. I think you have to ask Him from a humbled, maybe even broken heart, to get still enough to get your answer from Him.

It is awesome how things all work for good when God is put first. When we listen to Him and follow His instruction! I know there was a certain group within my own church that thought the ministry would surely fail. They would speak in secret that I wasn't that involved in enough church activities, I wasn't involved in children's ministry, my husband was not attending with me and so on, but I always said, "It is not my ministry, it is His, and nothing He creates can fail." What did it matter all those other things? Only He can take it away if the heart He puts it in isn't giving Him the glory, but it just can't fail when you keep your eye on that focus... His focus! And I gave Him the credit, the glory and the justification.

Chapter 10: I have a purpose and a plan

When we serve others, we ARE essentially serving God, and that's what makes it all worth it. Quote by Autumn Ater.

I can't explain how, but God knew how we would be a great blessing added to the ingredients He has called for within this recipe that He has called *"A Hole in My Heart Ministry!"* He had a purpose and a plan long ago, and knew that this would come to fruition. I am not always one to "follow the rules" and I had never remembered hearing God speak to me before, but I knew that there was something different about the night He planted the seed. By being obedient and following His lead, a wonderful ministry was born and is now reaching women all over the USA and abroad. God chooses different people for different missions, if you will, and this was truly my calling. When you are in doubt that God can use you for something truly amazing, that is Satan whispering insecurities into your head. Listen to your heart instead, take the leap of faith He asks of you and move forward. Great things will begin to happen.

You might be asking, why would He use you? How could He have a purpose and a plan for you? Perhaps you were as I was; not feeling as faithful as I knew I should have, or punishing myself for past things and even present ones… but God is awesome! He knows the one thing about us that cannot lie; our heart! He knows that we all sin and fall short, yet

He still entrusts us with certain tasks. Why miss the blessing?

From the book, *Grief and Loss*, by Katherine Walsh-Burke: *"Look well into thyself. There is a source of strength which will always spring up if thou will always look there."* —Marcus Aurelius.

"That which is important can only be felt within the heart." —Helen Keller.

How beautiful are those words. God can put those purposes (words) into your heart and you can feel the strength of listening to your thoughts, which could very well be the plans He is whispering into your soul. I promise you this, there is no greater joy than to serve others. It is healing and rewarding and can change everything about how you feel and perceive things in your life—even that of loss. So why be so frightened to open your heart up to God? He will give you step-by-step instructions for the purposes He has set out before you, and when you do the human thing and try to get ahead of Him, He will urgently, but gently, pull back the reins and slow you down. There is no "I" in doing His work. You cannot do His work and claim the glory…lest he shut you down and swiftly! Yet, he is compassionate and patient enough to allow us to see things in His timing and the "ah-hah" moments come to life.

I do know this—you have to ask Him to show you His purpose and His plan for your life though. We are too stubborn as humans to consider that option many times and, therefore, we miss the mark, the calling, the blessing. He instructs us: *"Ask and it will be given to you; seek and you will find; knock and the door will be opened to you." Matthew 7:7.*

Here are some learning objectives by Kelly Henderson, a Sunday school teacher:

- Each person has great value to God.
- The purpose for every follower of Jesus is to be used by God and to be a Godly influence in the lives of others.
- God has given His children gifts to help others to see that He exists and He wants them to be a member of His family.
- We are to trust and obey God even when we don't understand our circumstances.

God created you and me. He tells us in His Word that He knit us together while we were inside our mother's wombs. (Psalm 139:13-15). He knows every little detail about us. He knows how many hairs we have on our heads. (Matthew 10:30). He knows what we like and what we don't like. He made each of us unique and there is no one created exactly like us in the whole world.

We live in a world that sometimes makes us think that we aren't special because we are not popular, pretty, athletic, or as smart as others. Our value to

God isn't based on any of those things. He loves us because He created us and placed us in this world for a purpose. His purpose for placing each one of us on this earth is to glorify Him and enjoy Him forever. We glorify God when we live a life that pleases Him and points others to Him. When we live that kind of life, we will enjoy God and all the blessings that come from Him.

Because God's purpose is for each of us to glorify Him and enjoy Him forever, He has given us gifts or talents that we can use to help others see that God exists and wants them to be a part of His family, too. You must remember this though...do not let Satan fill your head with lies. We all have a purpose and a plan and we are all vessels for HIM. You have many gifts that help others, and in doing so, you help God. My heart breaks for all the moms (myself included), but God planted this seed in my heart and I trust Him that He holds me together. We all walk this journey together and there is Joy and light at the end of the tunnel.

Sometimes we know clearly what our gifts/talents are and how God wants to use us in this life. Other times we may not know what our gifts and purpose are in this life. (If possible, take a gift-wrapped box out of a bag and set on your lap.) Our lives are like this unopened present. We have received a present but we don't know exactly what is inside until we take the wrapping paper off the present. As each of

Chapter 10: I have a purpose and a plan

us walk with God by faith day by day, obeying His Word, He begins to prepare us for what is inside that present. In God's perfect time, He allows the wrapping on the gift we have to come off and He allows us to see what the talent/ability for serving Him will be. Whether we know what gift God has given us or not, we are to live a faithful and obedient life that pleases God. Because even though we might not feel like we have a purpose and are not useful to God, He sees all that is going on around us. He knows how your life will affect the people around you.

We all influence the lives of others around us. No matter who we know, there is someone who is affected by the way you live your life. The question we need to think about is this: are you influencing people to want to know God and live for Him, or are you influencing people to disobey and rebel against God?

I know God lives in my heart and there is purpose there, along with joy in serving others. How wonderful that I am able to share my son's life and death and help another through it all. These are opportunities I prefer not to miss out on. I know it's a painful journey to even open the cover of the book of my grief and allow others in, but I also know that there is hope and a great sense of peace in how someone reacts to my story and testimony. Being able to do all that I do is not easy by any means. I certainly have my moments that I don't want to share my loss and keep the thoughts of what we have been through private within myself, but when I do share and look up into the eyes of another and see tears—tears that they are shedding for me and my son—I know I have struck a deep chord within them and have opened a window into my world of grief. It is an instantaneous feeling of calm and all I want to do is comfort them now. Perhaps they needed to hear of the many trials we endured with Robert and how we hold true to our faith regardless of the pain we (and Robert) had suffered. God can use anyone, even me—this unlikely vessel—to reach another in a place that only He can open up. It is a blessing to share my son's life with you and it is in hope that you will come away with encouragement that all things really do work together for those who love God!

"Consider it pure joy, my brothers, when you face trials of many kinds." James 1:2.

Okay, to count our hurt, our pain and our struggle as nothing but pure joy? How can that be? This is how… *"And we know that all things God works for the best for those who love Him." Romans 8:28.*

That verse really spoke to my heart and convicted me to the point where I know there is no such thing as luck, chance or coincidence that bad things will happen in our life.

I had complete peace knowing that God won't let anything happen to us in our life unless He has a good purpose for it all.

I was given the wisdom to understand that if we pray for something, if it is God's will, it will happen in His time. If it's not God's will for it to happen, then I know that He has something better planned. I now see glory revealed as He is using me just the way I am and in ways others cannot be used. Whatever God wants me to do, and wherever He leads, I follow.

I have many dreams and goals that I have set to achieve in my life. I want to become the best witness I can be of God's love and hope and be used as a vessel in any place that He desires me to be. The opportunities and possibilities are endless with God in the obedient heart. I believe that if you have the desire and passion to do something, and if it's God's will, you will achieve it in good time. As humans, we continually put limits on ourselves for no reason at all. What's worse is putting limits on God who can do all things. We put God in a "box" and the awesome thing about the power of God is that we want to do something for God, but instead of focusing on our capability, we concentrate on our availability for we know that it is God through us and we can't do anything without Him. Once we make ourselves available for God's work, guess whose capabilities we now are relying on? God's! Now that's powerful food for thought.

I know it can be hard to expose these new feelings. We sometimes just get too relaxed and accepting of our pain and the thought of ever letting it go, is inconceivable. But we need to make those steps, take the chance so we can move again, live again and find peace, hope and joy. We will then wonder what we were so afraid of, not that grief isn't scary, because it sure it, but we cannot let it consume us. And don't blame yourself either if it seems too tough at first. That is Satan getting at you so you will avoid God and His love through this. I know a lot of the things people are saying to you make no sense right now, but in time you will start to feel differently…not that you will stop feeling for your loss, because you never will but just know how to better handle it. Don't let your grief identify who you are. Your child would not want you to do that. They are still very much a part of our every day existence, although unseen, they are felt. God walks this journey with you, too. He will never leave you and will place those in your life who can help or minister to you best. I am not as strong as many think. I just do my best to keep the faith, even when there seems to be none in sight. It's a process (grief) and one that will take all our earthly lives to endure!

Be the possibility that God wants you to be. Let Him guide you towards His purposes and plans for your life and watch the seeds sprout within!

Chapter 10: I have a purpose and a plan

"There are moments that mark your life,
Moments when you realize
Nothing will ever be the same.
And time is divided into two parts,
Before this
And after this."
Author Unknown

A Hole in My Heart—Finding Hope Through the Seasons of Change

CHAPTER 11
Forgiving grief by enduring it

*"We can rejoice, too, when we run into problems
and trials, for we know that they are good for us—
they help us learn to endure.
Endurance then develops strength of character in
us, and character strengthens
our confident expectation of salvation."*

Romans 5:3-5

To forgive grief by enduring it has become quite a statement by me. I was once asked to write a letter to grief, and the only thing I could write on the paper was, *"I forgive you by enduring you."* That was a hard assignment. How do you first write a letter to grief and then process the answer that was written? It was tough but we were asked to read aloud what we had written down, and so I read it. There was a lot of head nodding and "wow's"… the "I hadn't thought about it that way comments." Many, actually most, had written down things like, "I hate you grief, or you hurt too much. Leave me alone, I never asked you to come to my door." So to hear someone saying they had forgiven grief by enduring it, opened up a whole can of worms.

How do you forgive grief? I mean it's a part of everyday life and we all go through some form of grieving on a daily basis, but this was different to me. I was enduring this great loss, missing my son, not angry with God at all, but felt like I was holding onto my grief too tightly and the only way to let it not consume me was to forgive it. Isn't forgiveness for us anyway, I thought? I truly had to stop dragging it behind me everywhere I went. My life was becoming a daily struggle just to find any glimpse of joy and it all had to do with my grief; intense and justifiable as it was to me. I wanted to be free of this thing that was weighing me down. So, I let it go. I chose to forgive it and endure whatever I had to so I could move forward and not stand still anymore.

Grief can confuse you also…and make you do some rather strange things, too. I remember two very specific times that I had done something "so now hilarious" but was totally unaware of at the time. The first one was when I had gone through a Braums Restaurant & Ice Cream Store drive thru and ordered a Crabby Patty! She replied, "What?" and after three times of asking her for the same thing, the girl on the speaker box started cracking up and told me in a silly voice, *"Sorry, we don't serve them here, you can only get it at The Krusty Krab," under the sea where SpongeBob (the cartoon character) lives, but I could make you a nice junior cheeseburger instead if you like."*

Oh my goodness, I felt like such an idiot and embarrassed wasn't even the word, especially since I had asked for it all those times before she laughingly explained it to me. I was in *'lala'* land to say the least.

Another time, shortly after Robert's death, my husband and I took a little road trip to get out of town and away from all the stress. He asked me to keep a watch on the compass and be sure we were going north. I thought, "NO Problem. I can handle this!" But I had a concern after a while and wanted to talk to him about this compass that he had handed me, but we were getting lost and he was getting frustrated. I tried to speak up, but every time I even tried, he snapped, "Are we still going North?" and I would say yes, but...and he would cut me off. Finally he said angrily, "Which way are we going?" And of course, I said, "North." He never looked my way but just said, "Give me that dang compass. Something's wrong with it cause we are heading right into the sunset and I **KNOW** that is West." So I handed it to him and said ever so frankly and assuredly, "I tried to tell you everytime you asked me which way were we headed that something was wrong with it, because there is this little red needle thing moving all around it." He just **BUSTED OUT LAUGHING.** I, being the eastern-raised city girl I was, not knowing how to properly read a compass was holding the N in front of me, so no matter which way we were going, as long as N was in front of me, we were going North! He couldn't be mad and wasn't, but we both laughed hysterically and I now know how to read a compass with perfection. So see, you are not alone if you do goofy things. Grief makes us bonkers. I, up until recently, could only share that with certain people as I know I can never live it down, so consider yourself privileged that I have told on myself!

But you see, I am human, and we humans ... well, we make mistakes. I have had to forgive my husband a lot of times for embarrassing me with that old story that he told to everyone we met, but which I have to admit, now cracks me up, too. But there was a time I didn't want it repeated over and over again. Does this remind you of anything familiar? Yep, grief!

I guess then you could say that these trials you have to endure are good reminders that you are right in the middle of God's plan and will, and that makes Satan really mad! But by being forgiving and holding up under pressure can in the long run, bring a turnabout of how you see things; how you handle them.

I've also learned in grieving that crying is cleansing and is quite a blessing that God gives to us. If I could not shed the tears of my pain, I don't know what would happen to me. My heart would break and I don't think it could beat anymore, but as quoted by Pope John XXIII: *I have looked into your eyes with my eyes. I have put my heart near your heart.*

To me that says a lot. How many times do we really look into another's eyes and into the depths of their souls and put our hearts near another's? We get so consumed with our own lives and its happenings that we never know when we do glance another's way, just what it is they might be going through.

If it were not for hopes, the heart would break.
—Thomas Fuller.

Amen! We must have hope. Forgiving grief by enduring it can release you from the clutches of what can potentially harm you in the end. God is the only answer!

I was chatting with another mom in my group, Barbara Rice, who lost her daughter, Diana, less than a year ago and she shared with me that her own mother had lost two children, (Barbara's siblings). One died thirty years ago and one died just two years ago. As we were talking, she indicated that she did not know where her mother got her strength from, but noticed her mother was starting to put distances in her relationships lately. She knew her mother loved her dearly and they are close, but she could sense the deep pain her mother was suffering. Not for just that of her own children's losses, but for the loss of her daughter's child. Yet, even so, she spoke only encouraging words to Barbara.

I felt a deep compassion for them both; but especially her mother at this moment, and as I listened, God put these words into my mouth to say ...

Barbara, she sounds like a pillar of strength. God's light has been shining through her, and she illuminates the Love He has for others by holding her memories close...and it is only natural for her to fear getting too close to anyone again, but sounds like even if she wanted to she could not stay away long! No matter what the day brings, God is right there in it, and if Diana, my son Robert and your mother's children are with God, then THEY are here in it with Him. I could see how God's love was influencing her, and how no matter how deep the depths of Barbara's mother's losses were, she had chosen to forgive this intense grief, and allowed herself to not be bitter. She showed her daughter great strength and encouragement to face the harsh things of this world, with the hope of what was yet to come.

Another mom shared these words;

I am exhausted, not tired, not lazy, absolutely exhausted. To wear a necklace with my daughter's picture and have several people throughout the day ask about her is hard. To cry so sadly, then belly laugh in the same hour is confusing and the confusion is so tiresome. Emptying your suitcase and finding a small pink sock from a trip in another life, another time is heart wrenching. To speak to a counselor about your deepest emotions while she helps you pick through them, sort them out, it is just mind numbing. To dedicate your morning to prayer and to dive into the word of God so intimately, yes it is comforting, but it is not an easy task. The warfare spreads like wildfires and my armor just drags behind me...I am so tired. My head aches, my body is sore, and I feel as if I just left the battlefield, the realization of this is that the battle has only just begun.

Grieving is not for the weak. Tackling these emotions head-on everyday takes strength, it takes courage if you ever think that someone who grieves for another must be weak, you are so very wrong and I pray that you never have to experience tragedy of any sort.

The battle for me starts the moment my feet hit the floor upon awaking each morning. It takes all I can do to NOT go to the place that cripples me. You have to find ways to fight that battle, depression and heartbreaking sorrow every single day…no matter how long it has been, it's a daily journey.

I can tell you that honestly, God is the reason I can do what it is I have to do. Seriously, I just have to trust Him with all He has purposed for my life and you can see the amazing works He is doing in so many women's lives after such tragedy strikes. We know we are all broken up inside, but He lovingly places others into our lives to help put the pieces back together again. That is the awesome power of the God we serve.

> *May God, who gives this patience and*
> *encouragement, help you live*
> *in complete harmony with each other,*
> *as is fitting for followers of Christ Jesus.*
>
> *Romans 15:5*

by Sharon S. Key Southern

CHAPTER 12
Healthy grieving

I am leaving you with a gift—peace of mind and heart! And the peace I give is not fragile like the peace the world gives. So don't be troubled or afraid.

John 14:27

It can be very difficult to find the best way to grieve over your losses. Everyone grieves differently and there is no right or wrong way to grieve, but we must not let our grief identify us and over-take us; leading us to a life of depression, guilt, fear and so many other conditions and emotions. Loving yourself requires you to be truthful about your own feelings. If you are happy, acknowledge the joy. If you are sad, acknowledge the sorrow.

When you are truthful about your feelings, you do not try to lie to yourself or seek to bury your negative emotions. Instead, acknowledging what you feel provides a good guide to what your thoughts are. And as we all know, thoughts can be changed, so that healing and self growth can take place, so be truthful to yourself!

We all go through the motions with grief; it is a never ending roller coaster ride that quite honestly makes you feel sick—physically, emotionally, mentally and spiritually. We may find we need a little help, and that's okay. But we must be honest about how we are doing and what we are feeling.

I was recently told this by a dear friend and it goes like this:

I know we haven't been exactly in each other's shoes; but we've experienced feelings of hurt, pain and heartbreak. My prayer for you is to just continue to keep your eye on the prize. Like Paul says in Philippians, "press on." Satan wants so badly for us to meltdown and turn from God but we daily have to pick up our cross and follow Jesus.

It seems like the verse about "the trials of this present time are nothing to be compared to what is to come" keeps coming to mind. I pray God may bring comfort in that.

I couldn't agree more with her either. What a true statement. We all walk in the same "labeled" grief shoes, but they come in all different sizes, shapes, and styles. No two people will grieve alike. Men and women, for instance, grieve very differently. Women tend to lean more towards the feeling and emotion aspect of it. Whereas, men tend to lean towards the fact and logic of it. It does not mean that one cares more about the death than the other;

Chapter 12: Healthy grieving

it just means we are programmed differently in how to *handle* our grief.

Men need to be strong and the stable head of household, the provider if you will; whereas, women want to talk about their feelings over the loss all day long…every day! Men cannot do that. Their brains cannot handle the emotional ride. It's a head-on approach to reality for them. If they, who from the time they were small boys and taught to be tough, suck it up, be a big boy and don't, whatever you do, don't cry…start to falter, then the entire unit crashes in. So instead, they suppress any *feelings* and urge themselves to be "the man." Be the strength of the family because we women are the weaker sex, or so that's what they have been taught.

Often times, men will show their signs of grieving by other means such as pushing themselves harder at work, exhibiting anger more easily, staying away from the home more often, spending more time alone, taking on new projects, and so many other things just to keep themselves distanced from allowing themselves to be like, well…us!

We women, on the other hand, need to be expressing ourselves all the time….tears, outbursts, talking, talking and more talking! Seeking additional support and constantly telling ourselves we will never survive this. We seem to lose all basic instincts for a while, but happily they return (for most) after the first year. We are on this emotional wave that never really reaches the shore and we just float or drift along each day in wonder of how we will get through the next moment, let alone rest of our lives.

Grief is a process, it is not a program that you participate in and then just "recover" from…although you do uncover some important things about yourself as the burden lightens and you walk this journey. Some will find themselves taking on new ventures and others will just be coping with daily life as best they can, but we all change. It is no crime to find yourself at a place where you feel okay about yourself and your life again. God wants us to fulfill our purposes and we may find ourselves going in a totally different direction than before…and that's okay. You have to be open to life!

Memories are wonderful, a true blessing from God. Without them, we would be like empty oyster shells with no pearls; nothing special on the inside…but God created you for something more. You are special to Him and He will reveal things in His own timing to you as you seek Him and move forward. Believe me, there is no greater death than that of your child, and to imagine life without them in unbearable. But we must not dishonor them by selfishly NOT living our lives. Can you imagine what they would say to us if we could talk to them? They are joyfully anticipating our arrival one day, and know that which we do not yet know. We need to remember that we

Chapter 12: Healthy grieving

will be reunited one day and to think anything other is disheartening.

Please read this beautiful conversation between a child and God:

"Is that my mom and dad?"

"Yes, sweet child," God said and pulled the child unto his lap.

"Why are they crying?"

"They cry for you, My child," God answered as He wrapped His arms around the sweet little one.

"Why do they cry for me?" The child asked.

"Because they want to hold you in their arms."

"But instead, You hold me in your arms, huh, God?"

"Yes, my child," God said.

"Why does that make them sad? I like it in Your arms!"

"Because they love you very much, it can make a mommy's and daddy's heart sad when they don't get to hold their children—I know how it feels to watch My Child die."

"Have I died, God?"

"Just on earth, child."

"I don't feel dead. I feel very much alive! Watch how fast I can run!" The child crawled down from God's lap. *"Yes, precious one, you are fast,"* God clapped.

"Now watch me fly!" The child said as they soared high. *"You are amazing!"* God laughed.

The precious child settled back into the safety of God's arms and said, "When will my parents fly, God?"

"Someday... my child."

"Will we fly together?"

"Yes. My mark is on their foreheads."

"Good," said the child.

"Will you tell them I am safe and happy?"

"I will comfort them, my dearest child."

"Will they be happy again?"

"Yes child. They will heal."

"And someday we will all get to be with You, huh, God?"

"Yes, someday," God promised.

"I love you, God," the child said and snuggled close to God.

"I love you, too, sweet one," God said as He put His hand on their head.

Chapter 12: Healthy grieving

"Take good care of my parents until they fly!" said the child.

"I promise," God whispered.

But here is where you can do something that will help you in your darkest moments...you can find healing in reaching out to another. There is nothing more healing than helping others throughout your time of need.

I, too, have thought those same words. Who can raise my child better than me? Only Jesus! It's a bittersweet thing and sometimes I feel selfish for missing my own child so much because I am grieving my loss. Who am I to say he himself (my child) lost anything. He gained what we can only imagine and a glory we likely cannot fathom. Can you imagine your child sitting in Jesus' lap or with Him sitting in the most beautiful and softest meadow having this conversation, and many others? It is a precious thought indeed and one that keeps me going. I know I will be with my child again, the Bible is God's word and it clearly states that we will be reunited and known as we are known now. Amen!

So, to help healing begin, do as Joel Osteen says; *when in need...plant a seed!* Shift your focus from yourself towards others and out of your pain comes your purpose. When we are desperate and asking God how to heal us or help us, let Him show you what another needs and fulfill that instead. You are then planting a seed of healing for yourself. It is the shifting of focus off of your needs and onto another and concerning yourself with them that will begin a chain of events so miraculous and joyful. It is most rewarding to help others. I know first hand this to be true. I prayed to God to heal me of the pain of my loss when my son, Robert, passed away; and He said *"serve others."* I did just that and now find myself in a totally different place than I thought I would be in.

The generous will prosper; those who refresh others will themselves be refreshed. Proverbs 11:25.

Then your light will break forth like the dawn, and your healing will quickly appear; then your righteousness will go before you, and the glory of the Lord will be your rear guard. Then you will call, and the Lord will answer; you will cry for help, and he will say: Here Am I. Isaiah 58:8-9.

We can become prisoners of our loss or break free and learn how to be a blessing to others and, in turn, you will be blessed ten fold! God will watch every step you take, leading your direction towards one of great joy. Although the loss is always there, we must remember there is hope. He will comfort us and provide all we need.

I will turn their mourning into gladness. I will give them comfort and joy instead of sorrow. —Jeremiah 31:13.

Chapter 12: Healthy grieving

Don't blame yourself either if you stumble. That is Satan getting at you so you will avoid God and His love through this. I know a lot of the things people say to you can make no sense, but in time you will start to feel differently. Not that you will stop feeling for your loss, because you never will but just know how to better handle it. Don't let your grief identify who you are. Your child would not want you to do that. They are still very much a part of our everyday existence, although unseen, they are felt. God walks this journey with you and He will never leave you and will place those in your life who can help or minister to you best. I am not as strong as many think. I just do my best to keep the faith, even when there seems to be none in sight. It's a process (grief) and one that will take all our earthly lives to endure!

I know it can be hard to peel those layers away. We sometimes get too comfortable in our pain to even consider letting it go, but once we do step outside of the "comfort zone box," we feel lighter and able to move forward. We find the air is so much easier to breathe; then wonder why we ever waited so long.

By allowing God to move through us, comfort comes. Joy returns and life moves on. We will find our new normal and we will make a difference if we listen to His calling and follow through.

An analogy of healing...after the loss of a child:

It is anguish I could not feel and so I shut it down; and now I cannot shut it out anymore. God is tearing me and it really hurts. A friend of mine said she knew someone who had a horse and the horse was becoming lame because he had a bad wound that healed from the outside in, not the inside out. The vet had to tear it open again so it would heal properly. And yes, the reopening of something this painful hurts, we are exposing something that we do not want to deal with but you just need to be patient with yourself and trust in a higher power.

"If you tell yourself that you cannot heal, then you won't. Don't think Negative as that's just a big "0" (nothing), instead, think Positive with all of its +'s

(gain) and never let someone take away from who you are but let only those in who add to your character. Have an attitude of gratitude and let the small stuff slide!" —Quote by Autumn Ater.

I came across this next piece in my earlier days of grieving and found it to be so helpful and healing. You will really feel the power and love of God and what is yet to come.

"So many people imagine that death cruelly separates us from our loved ones. Even pious people are led to believe this great and sad mistake. When our loved ones die, they do not leave us. They remain. They do not go to some dark and distant place. They simply begin their eternity. We do not see them because we are still in the darkness of the world. But their spiritual eyes, filled with the light of Heaven, are always watching us as they wait for the day when we shall share their perfect joy, We are all born for Heaven and one by one, we end this life of tears to begin our life of love in endless happiness.

I have often reflected upon this beautiful truth and found it the greatest and surest comfort in time of mourning. A firm faith in the real and continual presence of our loved ones has brought the conviction and consolation that death has not destroyed them, nor carried them away. Rather it has given them life! A life with power to know fully and to love perfectly. With this new life and new power, our loved ones are always present to us, knowing and loving us more than ever before.

The tears that dampen eyes in time of mourning are tears of home-sickness, tears of longing for our loved ones. But it is we who are away from home, not they. Death has been for them a doorway to an eternal home. And only because this heavenly home is invisible to our worldly eyes, we cannot see them so near us. Yet, they are with us, lovingly and tenderly waiting for the day when we, too, shall enter the doorway of our eternal home.

No, death is not a separation. It is a preparation for eternal union with those we love, in the peace and joy of Heaven," by Rev. Charles Shelby, St. Mary's Seminary, Missouri.

... And surely I am with you always, to the very end of the age." —Matthew 28:20.

Before ending this book, I would like to include something from my first book, which I think is crucial in our healing process. I am glad that I could be here for you in whatever way God has purposed me to be—even if by helping ease just a bit of your pain and filling a small place in your heart. I am truly humbled to be that vessel for Him and you!

The trials we face in this life will one day fade when we, too, cross over to the Father. He only wants for us to be in a continual relationship with Him, to truly

Chapter 12: Healthy grieving

give us the desires of our heart. He is not a God of falsehood, but truth, and love. His truth can truly set you free.

If you have never known the Lord before, I pray that you will say this simple prayer and ask him into your life, for He yearns to have a relationship and fellowship with you. He longs for you to love him as he loves you, so please pray this prayer if you desire to have him as Lord of your life. I promise the life you now know will never be the same again:

Dear Lord,

I believe that you are the son of God and that you died on the cross for me and took my sins upon yourself, rose on the third day and ascended to Heaven to sit at the right hand of God so that I may have a relationship with Him. I thank you for your love for me. I ask you to forgive me for my sins and come into my heart and make your dwelling there. Teach me your ways Lord, and help me to keep the faith, even when I don't understand things that happen in my world...let me seek yours. I trust in you Lord, and I accept your gift of love and forgiveness. In Jesus name, Amen

> *"If you confess with your mouth, 'Jesus is Lord,' and believe in your heart that God raised him from the dead, you will be saved.*

> *For it is with your heart that you believe*
> *and are justified, and it is with your mouth*
> *that you confess and are saved.*
>
> *Romans 10:9-10*

If you prayed this prayer from your heart, God now dwells within you and nothing can separate you from His love or presence! Hallelujah!

It is my hope and prayer that this book will bring comfort, joy and peace, along with the presence of the Lord God almighty to all who read it.

> *Open your heart to Him, He will find a home*
> *there; if you will but only allow him entrance and*
> *residence. And there He will dwell for all of time*
> *with you, an ever present part of our being...*
>
> *"Through the Seasons of Change"*

Chapter 12: Healthy grieving

"Ask and it will be given to you;
seek and you will find;
knock and the door will be opened to you.

Matthew 7:7

*To everything there is a season,
a time to every purpose under the Heaven:
a time to be born, a time to die, a time to plant,
and a time to pluck up that which is planted;
A time to kill, and a time to heal,
a time to break down, and a time to build up;
A time to weep, and a time to laugh,
a time to mourn and a time to dance.*

Ecclesiastes 3:1-4

The Wailing of the Soul Cry

Deep within a grieving heart
there lies a special place,
Its purpose may seem strange at first,
but still there none the less.

It opens up the heart to see
that life may not seem fair,
For it's the wailing of the soul cry;
you'll find upon your face.

Once let out of its capture...
and the tears begin to flow,
A cry will come not known before
and your heart begins to race.

The tears flow deeply as they
are softly carried away,
In the wailing of the soul cry...
where you'll finally find some peace.

It comes upon you suddenly,
with an element of surprise,
Utter weakness
now replaced by inner strength.

A glimpse of what is yet to come
has passed before your face,
The wailing of the soul cry
has shown you God's Amazing Grace.

So when that time does come,
where tears you cannot keep,
Fall from the depths of painful hurts;
from one's own grieving heart.

The journey has not ended,
it has only just begun;
Yes, the wailing of the soul cry,
are "your" tears meant to weep.

And after all the droplets,
have washed away the pain,
You'll feel a blessing of love and peace
that only God can give

And the thought of your dear loved one,
is still there to remain,
It's in the wailing of the soul cry,
where you'll learn to live again.

Copyright © 2009-2012 by Autumn Ater
August 2, 2009
For Robert: 8/12/91 – 4/22/06

ABOUT THE AUTHOR

Writing is something that Autumn has always enjoyed, especially journaling and poetry. She spent many nights curled up in her bed as a young child with a flashlight under the covers writing in the dark as to not awaken her two sisters, whom she shared a bedroom with...and not get caught by her parents for being up when she should have been getting some sleep!

Autumn Ater

But, it was there that she found a way to express her thoughts, her dreams and the *what if's* of life. As a small child, she would pretend-play that she was a teacher, and write out lessons for her dolls. In her then child's mind, she would grade her make-believe essays (of which she was the one actually writing) and giggled when they all made 100's! Imagine that? She honestly thought that she would one day be a teacher, but soon learned as she grew older that God had another plan in mind, and she embraced His calling.

Autumn was raised in Englishtown, New Jersey, being the eldest of four children, in a beautiful rural area, not too terribly far from the coast she loves so much and where her family still resides today. She then moved to Arizona briefly before moving to Texas to pursue furthering her education. Autumn is an Honors graduate of Weatherford College, and is anticipating working towards her Masters Degree in Faith-Based Counseling.

While obtaining her Associates Degree, she served as one of the first in a newly started program at Weatherford College as a Student Ambassador and was an Officer in Phi Theta Kappa, serving as Vice President of Fellowship. She also earned a Social Work Assistant Certificate through a completion course while attending Weatherford College. She thoroughly enjoyed her time at college and took full advantage of all it had to offer her—and, she was well recognized by the Administrators and staff for her achievements.

Autumn has two birth children… one living daughter, Elaina, and one deceased son, Robert, as well as three step-daughters: Jennifer, Alisha and Jamie, that she loves deeply and thinks of as her own. She is grandmother to five grandsons and one granddaughter.

Robert regrettably lost his battle on this earth and went home to Heaven on April 22, 2006, due to complications related to his many disabilities. He was 14 years old and is deeply missed. But Autumn's faith holds strong that she will be reunited again one day!

Autumn has been happily married to her best friend and greatest supporter, Scott, for 24 years and resides in Weatherford, Texas. Robert was their only child together. The Ater's own a local family plumbing business and both do charity work within the community. They have a marriage that has withstood the tests of time and a complimenting strength that is evident when you are around them. They both enjoy good times spent visiting with family and the company of wonderful friends, and Autumn has the gift of song, which she shares as often as possible.

In May of 2007, Autumn founded *A Hole in My Heart Ministry, Inc.* and is humbled to lead a wonderful faith-based organization helping other mothers who have experienced the death of a child or children. She believes it is her true calling from God and greatest gift to share.

Autumn has been a guest speaker at many benefits, including: Disabled Crime Victims Association, Dallas Crimes Against Children Association of Texas, Cook Children's Palliative Care Conference, REACT of Weatherford Police Dept, The Christian Resource Center of American Airlines, Caring Friends, the Evergreen Club, and recently attended; along with 44 other Texas authors in a huge book signing event called *Books, Authors and All That*

Jazz at Weatherford College for its 10th Anniversary and final year. She is also scheduled for several private book store signing events!

Autumn has also spoken at many local churches and been interviewed on Christian Radio several times, local News stations, Cable TV shows, a live on-air show with a 95.9 The Ranch, a local country music station as a part of a fund raising event with 14 amazing Texas artists, and has been in several magazines and some noted authors' published books.

The "Fountain of Tears" is a statue of Mary holding Jesus atop a beautiful fountain and is an "open year round" sanctuary for all to see. This was an ongoing project that Autumn had worked on for four years for *A Hole in My Heart Ministry,* and is now completed, placed in the majestic and Holy gardens of Praise Pavilion (www.praisepavilion.org) which is located in Weatherford, Texas. Also, the beautiful tear streaks on Mary's face were not done by any human hand (and was even examined by a local priest and blessed for its authenticity) but what we believe to be an anointed gift from God ... and how appropriate for this particular tribute.

About the Author

The Fountain of Tears

Mary's "God Gifted" Tear Tracks

The Fountain of Tears and Prayer Walk

A Hole in My Heart has become Autumn's passion as she serves other mothers whose hearts are broken from the loss of a child or children with healing by word and deed from an awesome God, and with the truth, knowledge and confidence that He walks this journey with them.

With the guidance of a Father she loves so much, Autumn's greatest prayer is to see this ministry grow as God has ordained; to continue being a vessel for Him as He leads her in ministry and that of serving others.

Autumn's first book, *"A Hole in My Heart ~ Finding Peace in God's Special Place"* first became available in March of 2012 and has been a huge success. Copies of this book are currently available at: www.aholeinmyheartbooks.com, but soon all books will be available from Amazon, Barnes & Nobles and many more stores and sites. She is most gracious and humbled for all of the support it has received. This is her second book in the *"A Hole in My Heart"* series to be published and she is anxious to see where God leads her next!

Autumn's favorite saying is simply this... *"God always has a Purpose and a Plan."*

> *The LORD is my strength and my shield;*
> *my heart trusts in him, and he helps me.*
> *My heart leaps for joy, and with my song*
> *I praise him.*
>
> *Psalm 28:7*

ABOUT "A HOLE IN MY HEART MINISTRY"

A Hole in My Heart Ministry is a Not for Profit, 501 C3 Organization offering support, comfort and understanding to mothers locally, nationally and internationally. Founded in 2007 by Autumn Ater, after the death of her son, Robert, in April 2006, it has grown to become one of the most recognized ministries by mothers, and is one of the few faith-based support groups for bereaved mothers to attend.

With the support of the community it serves, along with many other outreach programs, this fully non-paid staff of board members continues to reach out and offers compassion and resources to grieving mothers; along with some fantastic resources for grieving fathers. The ministry operates solely on in-kind and memorial donations, and there is a link on the website where you can help us to continue helping these precious mothers.

Using God's Word and by deed, our mission here is to open the door to healing the broken heart of mothers whose child or children have passed on ahead of us.

Grief from death is a powerful emotion that none can escape. We will all have to deal with the loss of a loved one at one point or another during our lifetime....but to a mother who has suffered the loss of her child or children, this grief can become overwhelming and consuming.

With other mothers to share with, *A Hole in My Heart* offers a safe and cozy place where we are free to discuss the memories of our child without any hesitation. A place to laugh, cry, pray together and feel a connection that only another mother who wears those shoes can relate to, and where we are reminded that death to a Christian is life eternal through Jesus Christ, our Lord and Savior.

A Hole in My Heart Ministry meets the second Thursday of each month and is about to open a second meeting location in the Dallas-Fort Worth area within the next few months. The ministry also offers a quarterly newsletter to its members, of which there is no charge for any of the services we provide. Again, if you would like to be a part of contributing to our efforts by making a tax-free donation, please visit our website www.aholeinmyheart.com or contact us for further information on ways you can help.

Finally, we ask that you please pray for this group so that if (and when) this unfortunate occasion arises; you can make referrals in confidence that they are

About "A Hole in My Heart Ministry"

not alone. We are here to listen. We are here to rely on God's strength to help carry this burden….and find joy once again.

Blessed be His Holy Name!

> *"He will wipe away every tear from their eyes.*
> *There will be no more death or mourning*
> *or crying or pain, for the old order*
> *of things has passed away."*
>
> *Revelation 21:4*

I Miss You

Each morning when I wake up
My first thought is of you;
Are you happy up in Heaven?
Your body made anew.

Do you play with other children?
And have quiet talks with God?
Walking hand in hand with Jesus
Where all the Angels trod.

How I miss your precious smile
And the twinkle in your eyes;
As I look up into Heaven
In a bright and star filled sky.

I wish that I could see you
And in the memory of my mind;
You're flying high across the Heaven's
Until the end of time.

I know we'll be together
Surrounded by God's love;
Where flying all around us
Will be angel's up above.

Our dear departed loved ones
Will be forever at our side;
No more tears or empty sorrows
For in His love we'll all abide.

About "A Hole in My Heart Ministry"

I miss you so my heart breaks
With every beat it makes;
Yet the comfort in God's promise
Is all it ever takes.

To know that God had chose me
To care and tend to you;
To love you and to keep you
Until your time was through.

Now I wait upon my calling
To join you in His grace;
In a grand and glorious home
Yes, Heaven be the place.

There are no other words
To express all that I feel;
I promise that I miss you
And that you know is real.

I will always keep on loving
And forget you I will not;
But God will heal my broken heart
And fill the hole I've got.

Please know that I have longed
To hold you close to me;
Someday up in the Heavens
It will happen, you will see.

You are so precious to me
And forever I'll love you;
I'll miss you every second
And this I promise you.

That someday we'll meet again
In the glory of God's Love;
In a home that we'll call Heaven
Far up in the sky above.

So when I think of you now
I will know that you are there;
Watching over me with gladness
And tender loving care.

Everyday I ask God to tell you
That I love and miss you so;
And to keep you real close to me
Because I never wanted you to go.

But God's great plan was finished
Yes, all your time was through;
And all I can do now
Is forever just miss you.

I Miss You!!!!!

Copyright © 2012, Autumn Ater, June 9, 2006;
In Memory of Robert; August 12, 1991 – April 22, 2006.

SCRIPTURE INDEX

*Now that you have purified yourselves
by obeying the truth so that you have sincere love
for each other, love one another deeply,
from the heart.*

Peter 1:22

*What is your life? It is even a vapor
that appears for a little time
and then vanishes away.*

James 4:14

*For you created my inmost being;
you knit me together in my mother's womb.
I praise you because I am fearfully
and wonderfully made; your works are wonderful,
I know that full well. My frame was not hidden
from you when I was made in the secret place.
When I was woven together in the depths
of the earth, your eyes saw my unformed body.
All the days ordained for me were written
in your book before one of them came to be.*

Psalm 139:13-16

*Dear friends, do not be surprised at the painful trial
you are suffering, as though something
strange were happening to you. But rejoice
that you participate in the sufferings
of Christ, so that you may be overjoyed
when his glory is revealed.*

1 Peter 4:12-13

In Christ, all things are made new again.

2 Corinthians 5:17

*O LORD, you have examined my heart
and know everything about me.
You know when I sit down or stand up.
You know my thoughts even when I am far away.
You see me when I travel and when I rest at home.*

*You know everything I do. You know what
I am going to say even before I say it, LORD.
You go before me and follow me.
You place your hand of blessing on my head.*

*Such knowledge is too wonderful for me,
Too great for me to understand!
I can never escape from your Spirit!*

*I can never get away from your presence!
If I go up to Heaven, you are there;
If I go down to the grave, you are there.*

*If I ride the wings of the morning,
if I dwell by the farthest oceans,
even there your hand will guide me,
and your strength will support me.*

*I could ask the darkness to hide me
and the light around me to become night,
but even in darkness I cannot hide from you.
To you, the night shines as bright as day.
Darkness and light are the same to you.*

*You made all the delicate, inner parts of my body
and knit me together in my mother's womb.
Thank you for making me so wonderfully complex!*

*Your workmanship is marvelous—
how well I know it. You watched me
as I was being formed in utter seclusion,
as I was woven together in the dark of the womb.
You saw me before I was born.*

*Every day of my life was recorded in your book.
Every moment was laid out before a single day had
passed. How precious are your thoughts about me,
O God. They cannot be numbered! I cannot even
count them; They outnumber the grains of sand!
And when I wake up, You are still with me!*

Psalm 139: 1-18

Be not afraid, only believe.

Mark 5:36

*...to be made new in the attitude of your minds;
and to put on the new self, created to be like God
in true righteousness and holiness.*

Ephesians 4:23-24

*In the same way, the Spirit helps us
in our weakness. We do not know what we ought to
pray for, but the Spirit himself intercedes
for us through wordless groans.*

Romans 8:26

The Lord of hosts is with us.

Psalm 46:7

*So do not fear, for I am with you;
do not be dismayed, for I am your God.
I will strengthen you and help you;
I will uphold you with my righteous right hand.*

Isaiah 41:10

*Let them be like chaff before the wind,
with the angel of the Lord driving them away!*

Psalm 35:5

*Since we, God's children, are human beings,
made of flesh and blood, he became flesh and blood,
too, by being born in human form;
for only as a human being could he die
and in dying break the power of the devil
who had the power of death. Only in that way could
he deliver those who through fear of death have
been living all their lives as slaves
to constant dread.*

Hebrews 2:14-15

*Having loved His own who were in the world,
He loved them to the end.*

John 13:1

*To every thing there is a season,
and a time to every purpose under the Heaven...
a time to mourn and a time to dance.*

Ecclesiastes 3:1,4

*Hear, O LORD, and be merciful to me;
O LORD, be my help." You turned my wailing
into dancing; you removed my sackcloth
and clothed me with joy, that my heart may sing
to you and not be silent. O LORD my God,
I will give you thanks forever.*

Psalm 30:10-12

*There is a time for everything, and a season
for every activity under Heaven: a time to be born
and a time to die, a time to plant
and a time to uproot, a time to kill
and a time to heal, a time to tear down
and a time to build, a time to weep
and a time to laugh, a time to mourn
and a time to dance, a time to scatter stones
and a time to gather them, a time to embrace
and a time to refrain, a time to search
and a time to give up, a time to keep
and a time to throw away, a time to tear
and a time to mend, a time to be silent
and a time to speak, a time to love
and a time to hate, a time for war
and a time for peace. What does the worker gain
from his toil? I have seen the burden God has laid
on men. He has made everything beautiful
in its time. He has also set eternity in the hearts
of men; yet they cannot fathom
what God has done from beginning to end.*

Ecclesiastes 3:1-11

*He will wipe every tear from their eyes.
There will be no more death or mourning
or crying or pain, for the old order of things
has passed away.*

Revelation 21:4

*Not only so, but we also glory in our sufferings,
because we know that suffering produces
perseverance; perseverance, character; and
character, hope. And hope does not put us to shame,
because God's love has been poured out
into our hearts through the Holy Spirit,
who has been given to us.*

Romans 5:3-5

*...and teaching them to obey everything
I have commanded you. And surely I am with you
always, to the very end of the age.*

Matthew 28:20

... Never will I leave you; never will I forsake you.

Hebrews 13:5

*He himself bore our sins in his body on the tree,
so that we might die to sins and live for
righteousness; by his wounds
you have been healed.*

1 Peter 2:24

*Every day of my life was recorded in your book.
Every moment was laid out
before a single day had passed.*

Psalm 139:16

*To be absent from the body
is to be present with the Lord.*

2 Corinthians 5:8

It is impossible for God to lie.

Hebrews 6:18

*But you, O Lord, are a compassionate
and gracious God, slow to anger,
abounding in love and faithfulness.*

Psalm 86:15

*By this I know that thou favourest me,
because mine enemy doth not triumph over me.*

Psalm 41:11

*Do not let your hearts be troubled.
You believe in God; believe also in me.
My Father's house has many rooms;
if that were not so, would I have told you
that I am going there to prepare a place for you?
And if I go and prepare a place for you,
I will come back and take you to be with me
that you also may be where I am.*

John 14:1-3

*Remember me with favor, my God,
for all I have done for these people.*

Nehemiah 5:19

For My yoke is easy and My burden is light.

Matthew 11:30

*Praise be to the God and Father
of our Lord Jesus Christ, the Father
of compassion and the God of all comfort,
who comforts us in all our troubles,
so that we can comfort those in any trouble
with the comfort we ourselves have received
from God. For just as the sufferings of Christ
flow over into our lives, so also through Christ
our comfort overflows.*

2 Corinthians 1:3-5

*And we pray this in order that you may live a life
worthy of the Lord and may please him in every
way: bearing fruit in every good work,
growing in the knowledge of God.*

Colossians 1:10

*And whatever you do, in word or deed, do
everything in the name of the Lord Jesus, giving
thanks to God the Father through him.*

Colossians 3:17

*And let us consider how to stir up
one another to love and good works.*

Hebrews 10:24

*...For it is God who works in you,
both to will and to work for his good pleasure.*

Philippians 2:13

*Show yourself in all respects to be a model
of good works, and in your teaching
show integrity, dignity, and sound speech
that cannot be condemned, so that an opponent
may be put to shame, having nothing evil to say
about us. Slaves are to be submissive
to their own masters in everything;
they are to be well-pleasing, not argumentative.*

Titus 2: 7-9

*But the anointing that you received from Him
abides in you, and you have no need
that anyone should teach you.*

*But as his anointing teaches you
about everything, and is true,
and is no lie—just as it has taught you,
abide in him.*

1 John 2:27

*So in everything, do to others
what you would have them do to you,
for this sums up the Law and the Prophets.*

Matthew 7:12

*Love the Lord your God with all your heart
and with all your soul and with all your mind
and with all your strength.
The second is this: Love your neighbor as yourself.
There is no commandment greater than these.*

Mark 12:30-31

The Beatitudes

*Blessed are the poor in spirit,
for theirs is the kingdom of Heaven.
Blessed are those who mourn,
for they will be comforted.*

*Blessed are the meek,
for they will inherit the earth.
Blessed are those who hunger and thirst
for righteousness, for they will be filled.*

Blessed are the merciful,
for they will be shown mercy.
Blessed are the pure in heart,
for they will see God.

Blessed are the peacemakers,
for they will be called children of God.
Blessed are those who are persecuted
because of righteousness, for theirs
is the kingdom of Heaven.

"Blessed are you when people insult you,
persecute you and falsely say all kinds of evil
against you because of me. Rejoice and be glad,
because great is your reward in Heaven,
for in the same way they persecuted
the prophets who were before you.

Matthew 5: 3-12

For the LORD is good and his love endures forever;
his faithfulness continues through all generations.

Psalm 100:5

Love the LORD your God with all your heart
And with all your soul and with all your strength.

Deuteronomy 6:5

*I tell you the truth; anyone who will not
receive the kingdom of God like a little child
will never enter it.*

Luke 18:17 and Mark 10:15

*Brothers and sisters, we do not want you
to be uninformed about those who sleep in death,
so that you do not grieve like the rest of mankind,
who have no hope. For we believe that Jesus
died and rose again and so we believe that God
will bring with Jesus those who have fallen asleep
in him. According to the Lord's word,
we tell you that we who are still alive,
who are left until the coming of the Lord,
will certainly not precede those
who have fallen asleep. For the Lord himself
will come down from Heaven,
with a loud command, with the voice
of the archangel and with the trumpet call of God,
and the dead in Christ will rise first.
After that, we who are still alive and are left
will be caught up together with them in the clouds
to meet the Lord in the air. And so we will be
with the Lord forever. Therefore, encourage
one another with these words.*

I Thessalonians 4:13-18

Where, O death, is your victory?
Where, O death, is your sting?

1 Corinthians 15:55

Stand up and praise the LORD your God,
who is from everlasting to everlasting.
Blessed be your glorious name, and may it be
exalted above all blessing and praise.
You alone are the LORD. You made the Heavens,
even the highest Heavens, and all their starry host,
the earth and all that is on it, the seas
and all that is in them. You give life
to everything, and the multitudes
of Heaven worship you.

Nehemiah 9:5-6

For I will turn their mourning into joy,
And I will comfort them,
and give them joy for their sorrow.

Jeremiah 31:13

For I know the plans I have for you,
declares the LORD, plans to prosper you
and not to harm you, plans to give you hope
and a future.

Jeremiah 29:11

*Ask and it will be given to you;
seek and you will find;
knock and the door will be opened to you.
Matthew 7:7*

*He tells us in His Word that He knit us together
while we were inside our mother's wombs.*

Psalm 139:13-15

*He knows every little detail about us.
He knows how many hairs we have on our heads.*

Matthew 10:30

*Consider it pure joy, my brothers,
when you face trials of many kinds.*

James 1:2

*And we know that all things God works
for the best for those who love Him.*

Romans 8:28

*We can rejoice, too, when we run into problems and
trials, for we know that they are good for us—
they help us learn to endure. Endurance then
develops strength of character in us, and character
strengthens our confident expectation of salvation.*

Romans 5:3-5

*May God, who gives this patience
and encouragement, help you live
in complete harmony with each other,
as is fitting for followers of Christ Jesus.*

Romans 15:5

*I am leaving you with a gift—peace of mind
and heart! And the peace I give is not fragile
like the peace the world gives.
So don't be troubled or afraid.*

John 14:27

*The generous will prosper;
those who refresh others
will themselves be refreshed.*

Proverbs 11:25

*Then your light will break forth like the dawn,
and your healing will quickly appear;
then your righteousness will go before you,
and the glory of the Lord will be your rear guard.
Then you will call, and the Lord will answer;
you will cry for help, and he will say: Here Am I.*

Isaiah 58:8-9

*I will turn their mourning into gladness.
I will give them comfort and joy
instead of sorrow.*

Jeremiah 31:13

*... And surely I am with you always,
to the very end of the age.*

Matthew 28:20

*If you confess with your mouth, 'Jesus is Lord,'
and believe in your heart that God raised Him
from the dead, you will be saved.
For it is with your heart that you believe
and are justified, and it is with your mouth
that you confess and are saved.*

Romans 10:9-10

*Ask and it will be given to you; seek
and you will find; knock and the door
will be opened to you.*

Matthew 7:7

A Hole in My Heart—Finding Hope Through the Seasons of Change

To every thing there is a season, a time to every purpose under the Heaven: a time to be born, a time to die, a time to plant, and a time to pluck up that which is planted; A time to kill, and a time to heal, a time to break down, and a time to build up;
A time to weep, and a time to laugh, a time to mourn and a time to dance.

Ecclesiastes 3:1-4

The LORD is my strength and my shield; my heart trusts in him, and he helps me. My heart leaps for joy, and with my song I praise him.

Psalm 28:7

He will wipe away every tear from their eyes. There will be no more death or mourning or crying or pain, for the old order of things has passed away.

Revelation 21:4

www.ingramcontent.com/pod-product-compliance
Lightning Source LLC
Chambersburg PA
CBHW060527100426
42743CB00009B/1448